MW01485364

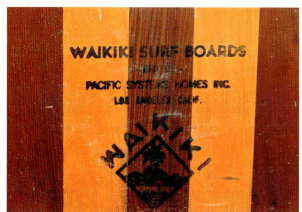

WAIKIKI SURF BOARDS

PACIFIC SYSTEMS HOMES INC.

LOS ANGELES, CALIF.

WAIKIKI

Hobie

SURFBOARDS
DANA POINT, CALIF.

They that go down to the sea in ships, that do business in great waters: these see the works of the Lord, and His wonders of the deep. For he commandeth and raiseth the stormy wind, which lifteth up the waves thereof. They mount up to the heavens, they go down again to the depths: their soul is melted of trouble.

—Psalm 107: 23-26

"Every day of the year where the water is 76, day and night, and the waves roll high, I take my sled, without runners, and coast down the face of the big waves that roll in at Waikiki."

—Hawaiian surfing hero Duke Kahanamoku

"All I need are some tasty waves and a cool buzz and I'm fine."

—Sean Penn as quintessential surfer dude Jeff Spicoli, *Fast Times at Ridgemont High*, 1982

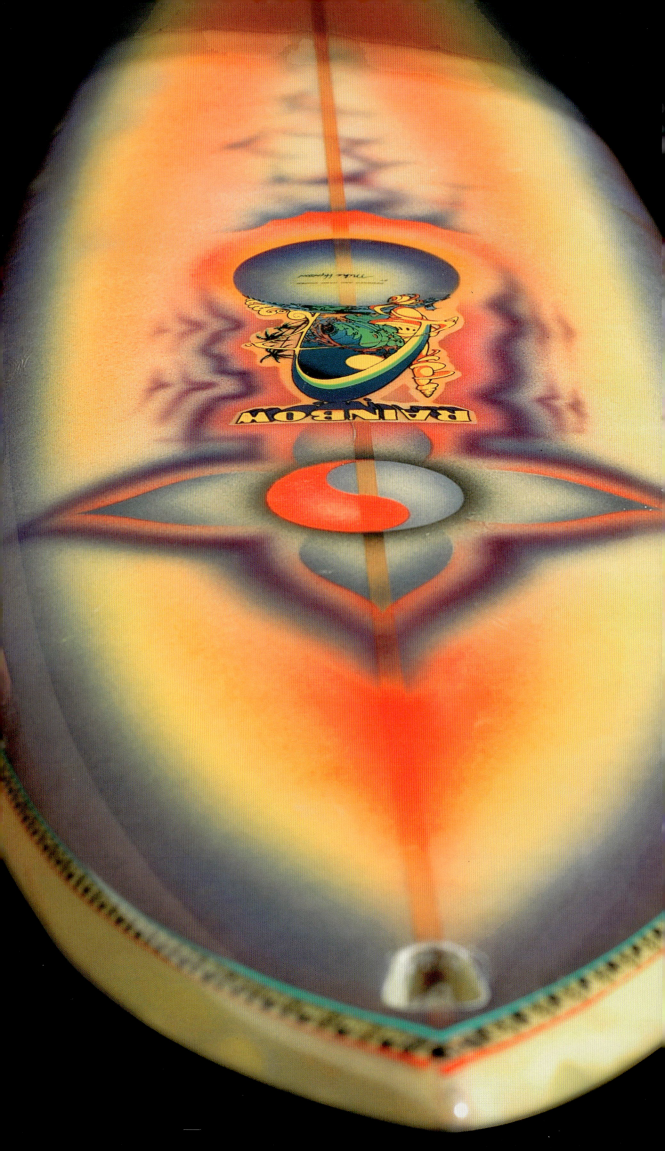

The Surfboard
Art · Style · Stoke

Duke Kahanamoku
Hawaiian Swimmer

DUKE

By Ben Marcus
Surfboard Photography by Juliana Morais
Surfing Photography by Jeff Divine
Surfboards from the Fernando Aguerre Collection
Foreword by Gary Linden

MVP
BOOKS

First published in 2007 by Voyageur Press, an imprint of MBI Publishing Company, 400 First Avenue North, Suite 300, Minneapolis, MN 55401 USA

Copyright © 2007, 2010 by Ben Marcus

Hardcover edition published in 2007.
Softcover edition 2010.

All rights reserved. With the exception of quoting brief passages for the purposes of review, no part of this publication may be reproduced without prior written permission from the Publisher.

The information in this book is true and complete to the best of our knowledge. All recommendations are made without any guarantee on the part of the author or Publisher, who also disclaims any liability incurred in connection with the use of this data or specific details.

We recognize, further, that some words, model names, and designations mentioned herein are the property of the trademark holder. We use them for identification purposes only. This is not an official publication.

MVP Books titles are also available at discounts in bulk quantity for industrial or sales-promotional use. For details write to Special Sales Manager at MBI Publishing Company, 400 First Avenue North, Suite 300, Minneapolis, MN 55401 USA.

To find out more about our books, visit us online at www.mvpbooks.com.

ISBN-13: 978-0-7603-3886-5

Editor: Michael Dregni
Designer: Sara Grindle

Printed in China

The Library of Congress has cataloged the hardcover edition as follows:
Library of Congress Cataloging-in-Publication Data

Marcus, Ben, 1960–
  The surfboard : art, style, stoke / by Ben Marcus ; surfboard photography by Juliana Morais ; surfing photography by Jeff Divine ; surfboards from the Fernando Aguerre Collection.
      p. cm.
  Includes index.
  ISBN-13: 978-0-7603-2753-1 (hc w/ jacket)
  ISBN-10: 0-7603-2753-X (hc w/ jacket)
  1. Surfboards—History. 2. Surfboards—Collectibles. 3. Surfing—History. I. Title.
GV840.S8.M27 2007
797.3'2—dc22

2006101365

On page 1: *Surfboard details then and now.*

On page 3: *"Surf Swimming by Sandwich Islanders," an 1870s engraving from the Reverend J. G. Wood's guidebook,* The Uncivilized Races of Man in All Countries of the World. *Voyageur Press Archives*

On pages 4 and 5: *Bruce Irons explores the technological advances of the modern plastic fantastic surfboard. Highly refined, super-light surfboards with low foam volume, light glass jobs, and three fins give today's surfers wings to fly.* Photograph © Jeff Divine

On page 4: *Mike Hynson Rainbow, 8'0", from the early 1970s.*

On page 5: *Swimming and surfing hero Duke Kahanamoku became an image of Hawai'i, promoted on postcards such as this one to be sent home to lure others to the Islands.* Voyageur Press Archives

Contents

Foreword

By Gary Linden

Shaper Gary Linden is the founder and owner of world-famous Linden Surfboards. He has also served as a judge on the world pro circuit as well as working with the Billabong Odyssey, searching for a rideable 100-foot wave.

Simon Anderson needed that back thruster fin to keep from spinning out as his big frame leveraged his turns. Dick Brewer painfully developed the modern gun to avoid the punishment a 20-foot wave can exact on the poorly equipped surfer. Bob Simmons' physical limitations necessitated lighter equipment, resulting in the use of aerospace fiberglass, Styrofoam, and epoxy resin construction. Joe Quigg and Matt Kivlin just wanted to make all that empty, perfect, California point surf at Malibu and Rincon a little more enjoyable, so they made boards that could turn and burn.

The essence of the surfboard is the custom nature of its being, always designed to fit a specific need, surfer, wave, or performance. The surfer/shaper starts the design journey with selfish motivations—his or her desire to surf beyond the present possibilities—and spends years upon years developing the skills necessary to allow ideas to manifest into tangible working creations.

On a 1983 surf trip to Hawai'i with team riders David Barr, Mike Lambresi, and Mark Price, Dick Brewer lent us his personal Waimea gun for what would be the first trip to the Bay for all four of us. For me, it was my first real 20-foot wave, and the board worked like magic. I returned home ecstatic, and the next time Dick showed up at my factory to shape, I asked him to make me a magic board of my own. In trade, I shaped him a four-fin for small waves. We had worked this way for years, trading our expertise for small-wave and big-wave designs to the betterment of us both. My first and last ride with it was at Waimea on my birthday, before the Billabong Pro that I judged later that day. Needless to say, the board was not as magical as the one he had made for himself. That's what I mean about selfish motivations.

But the reality is, it's difficult to make a custom surfboard for someone else. After about a year of garage shaping in the late 1960s, I journeyed to Australia and got to watch Bob McTavish shape a board for Wayne Lynch. As exciting as it was for a young kid halfway around the world to watch a master at his craft, the one thing that has stuck with me to this day is what I feel is the essence of the custom board. Bob had the surfer stand in front of the blank, arms extended over his head as he drew the board's outline around the guy's body shape. That was his way of making sure the shoe fit.

The quest for the ultimate performance surfboard requires the right materials and the right eye to select them. Balsa has been a favorite of mine since I started shaping the wood in Ecuador in the mid-1970s. Though it's not the lightest or the most technologically advanced material, its performance in big waves is incomparable.

Mike Diffenderfer was the one who taught me how to select the wood. I met him while surfing through France in the early 1970s, and he let me in on his method. I looked at the three boards he was making: one was light, one was of medium weight, and one was heavy. Upon further questioning, he told me the heavy one was for the factory's owner, Michel Barland, knowing that it would go on display and not be surfed. The medium-weight board was for Jackie Baxter, a top surfer of the day. And the extremely light board that was left was Mike's personal board. He told me it was "shaper's wood." Shaper's wood has been my personal preference ever since.

Performance-inspired designs have since evolved beyond wood. Technology enables creation, which in turns forces advancement of technology. In the early 1980s when shortboards needed to be at least a pound lighter than they were, I approached Gordon Clark to make what we called an ultra-light blank, where less foam was poured into the mold and allowed to expand, making it lighter. It worked great, but suddenly, the supply stopped. I went up to see him, and he told me that he couldn't make it anymore because there were too many rejects. Financially, risk didn't equal reward. I offered to buy all the rejects, seconds and firsts, if he would only keep making it. He agreed. With Clark's innovative foam, my boards were the lightest on the market, and before computerized shaping machines, we sold as many as our hands could make. Ultra-light soon became a shortboard industry standard, as Clark's production became more consistent.

But whatever the era or the technology, the seeds of innovation are often stored in the results of the past. New applications of old methods may result in new products. The Hawaiians who soaked their wood boards in mud were, in our modern language, actually giving them a ceramic seal. I think we need to revisit this approach. The next phase of surfboard evolution must be about returning to natural methods. Surfing is Nature's gift to us. In turn, we must protect Nature in any way we can. My next magic board will be 100% natural.

Surfer, shaper, designer, innovator—this book focuses on the most influential of the latter. From the earliest recorded surf-board designs to the present, the pictures are of the boards, not of their creators. In some way their life force has been mor-phed into something bigger than them-selves; the designs they have left forever record their time riding waves. Looking at the pictures, you can see the boards evolve. Laid out like this, the progression makes perfect sense. Where are we going? That will be determined by the waves we want to ride and how we want to ride them.

CHAPTER 1

Icons

Surfboards in Hawaiian Culture

1600 B.C. TO 1920 A.D.

E ven in the beginning, the surfboard was a religious icon. The early Hawaiians viewed their surfboards not just as recreational playthings but as tools for worshiping the ocean. Riding the ocean's energy was a reverential act, an integral part of the ancient religion of the Polynesian islands. And while surfing itself was not specifically a religious observance, as with all other aspects of Hawaiian life, it was connected to the gods.

The Polynesians had wandered for seventeen centuries from New Guinea through Polynesia to the middle of the Pacific. Whether by great seamanship or dumb luck—or a combination of the two—by 400 A.D., the first Polynesians came to this island chain they named "Owhyhee"—Homeland. Volcanic mountains rose above valleys where food grew in abundance, their revered ocean encircling all. The people of Owhyhee evolved in almost complete isolation for 1,300 years, before they were visited by outsiders in tall ships that might as well have come from Mars.

Princely Board, 1825
Prince Karimokou stands before his compound, his surfboard displayed front and center in this engraving from the book Iles Sandwich. *Bishop Museum*

Opposite Page:
***Olo*, 12'6"**
This solid koa *wood olo was shaped by Greg Noll as a tribute to the ancient Hawaiians. Only royalty were allowed to surf olos, and thus they were rare and special boards. This precious* koa *wood was hand-selected by Noll during a trip to Hawai'i, shipped to his California workshop, aged for two years, and then shaped. Adopted 2000.*

15

Surfing Nymphs, 1873
Hawaiian women ride the waves in this wood engraving from Charles Warren Stoddard's travelogue,
Summer Cruising in the South Seas. *Stoddard wrote of the surfers, "I watched the surf-swimming for some*
time, charmed with the spectacle." Bishop Museum

In July 1776, Captain James Cook left England on his third and final voyage. Cook's journey was a double fallacy, as he was seeking two items that didn't exist: the great Southern Continent and the Northern Passage. What Cook did find, beyond other things, was surfing. Observing a Tahitian wave rider, Cook wrote in his *Journals* in December 1777, "I could not help concluding this man felt the most supreme pleasure while he was driven on so smoothly by the sea."

When Cook stumbled on the northernmost Polynesian franchise, he found that supreme pleasure was deeply rooted in centuries of Hawaiian legend and culture. Place names were bestowed to honor and remember legendary surfing incidents. The Makahiki festival, an annual celebration to the god Lono, featured surfing rituals. The *kahuna* (priest) intoned special chants to christen new surfboards and to give courage to men and women who challenged the big waves. Hawaiians sang and chanted legendary stories of love matches made and broken in the surf, of lives risked, and of heroic ocean deeds by chiefs at the peak of the Sport of Kings.

To invoke the waves and speak to the ocean, surfers, led by the *kahuna*, gathered

Alaia, 7'9"

This solid koa board was shaped by Greg Noll in 1998. Alaia boards were surfed by Hawaiians into the twentieth century. For this board, Noll flew to Hawai'i to personally select the wood, shipped it home to California, aged it for more than one year, and then shaped it. Adopted 1998. Photograph by Larry Hammerness

on the beach and swung strands of *pohuehue* (beach morning glory) around their heads, thrashing the water while chanting in unison. One surf chant was recorded in the 1896 *Hawaiian Almanac and Annual*:

Kumai! Kumai! Ka nalu nui
mai Kahiki mai,
Alo po'i pu! Ku mai ka pohuehue,
Hu! Kai ko'o loa.

Arise! Arise, you great surfs from Kahiki,
The powerful curling waves,
Arise with *pohuehue*,
Well up, long raging surf!

Styles of Early Hawaiian Surfboards

Before contact with Cook, Hawaiians evolved a code of *kapu* (taboos) that regulated their lives: where to eat, how to grow food, how to predict weather, how to build a surfboard. There were reefs and beaches where the *ali'i* (chiefs) surfed and reefs and beaches where the commoners rode. Commoners generally caught waves on *paipo* (prone) and *alaia* (stand up) boards as long as 12 feet, while the *ali'i* rode waves on *olo* boards measuring up to an incredible 24 feet.

The ancient Hawaiian surfboard, or *papa he'e nalu* (pa-pa HAY-ay NA-lu), came in four types. Listed in order of length from longest to shortest, these were the superlong *olo* (O-lo), *kiko'o* (key-CO-oo), *alaia* (ah-LAI-ah), and *paipo* (pie-poe)

Proud Possession, 1890

A Hawaiian poses with his surfboard before his straw hut and his family. Photograph by T. Severin, Bishop Museum

not big. Yet the *olo's* limited maneuverability restricted use to breaks with easy swells and long rides.

For the majority of Hawai'i's steeper walls of water breaking closer to shore, the *alaia* was the better ride. Compared to the *olo* and *kiko'o*, the *alaia* was shorter, broader, less convex, and more planklike in its thinness. Surviving *alaia* boards range from 7 to 12 feet long, average 18 inches wide, and are from 1/2 to 1 1/2 inches thick. A representative *alaia* board was collected by J. S. Emerson in Kailua, Hawai'i, in 1885, and later donated to the Bishop Museum. Made of *koa*, it is 6 1/2 feet long and a little more than 1/2 inch thick at its center. The bow end is convex, the stern cut off square. Its widest point toward the nose is 14 3/4 inches while the narrower tail end is 10 3/4.

The *alaia* was best suited for *kakaha*, wrote Fornander, "a curling wave, terrible, death dealing"; that is, a wave that broke quickly and had a hollow curl. The board's short length and thinness made it preferable for a steeper, faster-breaking surf. And atop an *alaia*, Hawaiians perfected a technique called *lala* of sliding at an angle on the moving swell. As nineteenth-century historian John Papa Ii wrote, "On a rough wave, this board vibrates against the rider's abdomen, chest, or hands when they rest flat on it, or when the fingers are gripped into a fist at the time of landing. Because it tends to go downward and cut through a wave it does not rise up with the wave as it begins to curl over. Going into a wave is one way to stop its gliding, and going onto the curl is another. Skilled surfers use it frequently, but the unskilled are afraid of this board, choosing rather to sit on a canoe or to surf on even smaller boards."

bodyboard. The *olo* and *alaia* were both used under different surfing conditions and by different classes of people. The *olo* was typically 18 feet long and featured convex tops and bottoms tapered to thin, rounded edges; thus, either side appears to have worked as a riding surface. *Olo* boards were ideal for *opuu*, "a non-breaking wave, something like calmness," according to Abraham Fornander's *Hawaiian Folk Lore* of 1916–1920. Waves like this are typical at Waikiki on days when the surf is

Hawaiian Plank, 7'6"

This Hawaiian surfboard dates from 1895–1900, as certified by the Bishop Museum. This special board was unearthed during the clearing of a house lot on the North Shore. Adopted 2001.

Materials and Methods of Construction

Three different kinds of wood were used for the four types of Hawaiian surfboard. The *kiko'o*, *alaia*, and *paipo* boards were made from either *koa* (Hawaiian acacia) or *ulu* (breadfruit); the *olo* were made from the lighter wood of the flowering *wiliwili* tree, which was also used for outrigger canoes.

Of the three types of wood, commoners were denied the use of the best, *wiliwili*. As Duke Kahanamoku wrote: "They had to settle for the heavier, less buoyant, *koa* wood. It stood to reason then that the *ali'i* became

Hawaiian Redwood Surfboard, 8'10"
A stately and unrestored turn-of-the-century redwood "plank" from the shores of Waikiki. The board was found buried under an old house that was being torn down in Black Point, Oahu, near Waikiki. At one point it might have been painted, including the outline of a bull's head. The deck is flat, rolled up from the bottom rails. Adopted 2004.

the greatest surfers of those times. They certainly had every advantage. A man's board became a mark of his standing in society—sort of a status symbol."

Befitting its religious importance, *kapus* specified how surfboards were made. Kahanamoku explained, "The stages involved in selecting a proper tree, cutting it down, preparing the wood, treating it, and finally launching it as a finished surfboard, added up to a process that was fraught with labor, complexities and ceremonies. After proper blessings and incantations by the *kahuna* (priest) the tree was brought down and then trimmed of its branches preparatory for the final shaping. With only the assistance of stone or bone tools, the natives painstakingly shaped the wood into the desired proportions, then hauled it to their *helau* (canoe shed), where the prolonged, exacting work really began. Days of tedious scraping and cutting followed in order to obtain the wanted shape, depth, width and length. They strove for perfect balance, and sought to make the board fit the individual for whom it was intended. Each board was veritably custom-built and tailored to suit the 'wearer.' After countless hours of chipping with stone or bone adzes the board gradually took on the desired shape, and was then smoothed and polished by hand to the slickness that promised minimum traction and maximum maneuverability. The wood was then rubbed down with rough coral to erase the adze marks, and finally it was

Waikiki Beach Boys, 1910
Five Waikiki beach boys stand tall in front of their boards. Photograph by Ray Jerome Baker, Bishop Museum

polished with *'oahi* stone rubbers, all in the same way that the hulls of canoes were polished. *Kukui* nuts were then gathered and burned to a soot, and subsequently made into a dark stain. When applied to the wood, it brought out the fine grain and made the board a thing of shining beauty. In some instances the boards were stained a dark color with the root of the *ti* plant (*moke ki*). In others the natives resorted to making a stain from the juice of banana buds and charcoal from burnt pandanus leaves. In either case, when the stain became thoroughly dried, a preservative of *kukui* oil was rubbed in by hand, giving the surface an even glossier finish."

Applying the protective finish on the surfboard was an art in itself, as explained by Nathaniel Emerson in his 1892 article, "Causes of Decline of Ancient Polynesian Sports" for a journal called *The Friend*: "This Hawaiian paint had almost the

quality of lacquer. Its ingredients were the juice of a certain euphorbia, the juice of the inner bark of the root of the *kukui* tree, the juice of the bud of the banana tree, together with a charcoal made from the leaf of the pandanus. A dressing of oil from the nut of the *kukui* was finally added to give a finish."

Other ancient Hawaiian surfboard builders added another step in finishing boards. Twentieth-century surfboard innovator Tom Blake was the first modern surfer to restore traditional Hawaiian surfboards. He was told by Ken Cottrell, who witnessed this procedure, that a surfboard made of *wiliwili* was sometimes "buried in mud, near a spring, for a certain length of time to give it a high polish . . . The mud entered the porous surface of the *wiliwili* board acting as a good 'filler' for sealing up the surface. When the board was then dried out the mud surface became hard

Hawaiian Redwood
Waikiki Surfboard, 9'10"

This classic old-style surfboard once belonged to Buffalo Keaulana and dates from about 1910. While drinking beer at a picnic table at Buffalo's home in Nanakuli, Greg Noll saw youngsters Brian and Rusty Keaulana playing in the yard as if they were surfing, standing atop the old board. Noll told Buffalo he'd trade him a case of beer for the board. Keaulana's reply, "Take 'em, brada." The board has remained with the Noll family ever since. Several of the older Waikiki Beach boys dated the board back to around 1910. It was part of the old Queens surf fence. Adopted 2004.

and was polished and oiled to a fine water-proof finish."

Before it was launched, a surfboard received a dedication ceremony. Kahanamoku explained, "With the board ultimately ready for launching, the native *kahuna* administered more rites, dedicating it with special prayers. By the time the surfer took the board into the water, it had taken on a personality and significance which enlisted reverence from its owner. After use in the surf, the board was always left in the sun until wholly dry, then rubbed well with coconut oil, and hung up inside the *hale* (house). In fact the more exacting surfer even wrapped the board in *tapa* cloth to further protect and preserve the wood."

The Missionary Position

By the time Cook reached Hawai'i, the religion of surfing had reached a peak that was about to break. In the wake of Cook's ships *Resolution* and *Discovery*, Hawai'i and Hawaiian surfing fell into decline for more than 150 years. European, or *haole*, contact was not good for the islands, as they became the destination of choice for captains, brigands, adventurers, missionaries, and other opportunists. The *haole* brought new technologies and new gods, along with vices and diseases that savaged

Hawaiian Redwood Plank, 4'7"
This original, solid redwood board dates from the late 1910s. It is 18 inches wide with rolled rails and a typical period shape. Adopted 2001.

and ravaged Hawaiian society with a gentle genocide.

The undermining of Hawaiian culture accelerated in 1820 when Calvinistic Christian missionaries first arrived from New England and began to convert the Hawaiians from polytheism to their one god. Within a decade, the church's strict, moral Christian code was replacing the *kapu* system and the sensual Hawaiian way of life. Calvinists insisted the Hawaiians wear more clothes, learn to read and write English, work more, play less. And restrictions on play included banning surfing. As the Reverend Hiram Bingham, one of the staunchest defenders of the missionary position wrote: "The decline and discontinuation of the use of the surfboard, as civilization advances, may be accounted for by the increase in modesty, industry and religion."

Despite the imposed Calvinistic morality, surfing didn't disappear altogether from Hawai'i in the 1800s. While not practiced as widely, relentlessly, and religiously as when Europeans first arrived, surfing survived in the islands. And at times, even an adventurous *haole* would catch a wave, sit on top of the world, and then tell the world all about it. Mark Twain sailed to Hawai'i and rode a break—almost. He described his misadventure in his 1866 memoir *Roughing It*: "I got the board placed right and at the right moment, too; but missed the connection myself. The board struck the shore in three-quarters of a second, without any cargo, and I struck the bottom about the same time, with a couple of barrels of water in me."

To resurrect the Sport of Kings, a new breed of surfing royalty was needed.

Enter the Duke

As the twentieth century dawned, a freelance cinematographer named Robert Bonine survived the Yukon Gold Rush of 1896 and the San Francisco Earthquake of 1906 to trek to the Hawaiian Islands with something quite rare in those days—a kinetograph. Developed by Thomas Edison in 1888, the kinetograph was the earliest version of the movie camera.

The Hawai'i that Bonine came to film was now an annexed territory of the United States. Since Cook came to Hawai'i and was beaten and eaten, the native Hawaiian population had dwindled from an estimated 500,000 to just some 40,000, killed off by imported diseases, alcohol, and the depression of a vanquished race. Now, almost a third of the natives crowded together in or near Honolulu. The white *haole* settlers, however, were living the sweet life thanks to all that tariff-free Hawaiian sugar flowing out and all the money flowing in. Bonine arrived in Hawai'i the same year the Royal Hawaiian Hotel was built, as Hawai'i was beginning a long transformation from a sugar economy to tourism. And he saw and filmed a lot: *paniolo* on water horses

"Duke" Solid Redwood Plank, 10'6"
This tribute to Duke Kahanamoku was shaped by Greg Noll. Greg spent several days studying the original at the Bishop Museum in Hawai'i. It was shaped in 1996 from an ancient piece of redwood, one of fewer than twelve made. Adopted 1996.

Duke Kahanamoku, 1930s

Hawai'i's first surfing hero, Duke Paoa Kahanamoku stands with a towering olo in front of Waikiki Beach's Moana Hotel. Duke became the first star—and ambassador—of surfing, inspiring interest in the sport from Australia to California, and beyond. Photograph by Tai Sing Loo, Bishop Museum

The Kahanamoku Klan, 1905
Duke Kahanamoku stands with his brothers and another haole surfer, left, on Waikiki Beach.
Voyageur Press Archives

swimming cattle out to long boats; skinny, homesick Japanese sugar workers wrestling *sumo*; Honolulu Harbor full of steamships and tall ships; electric cars on the streets of the capital.

For one shot, Bonine stood on Waikiki beach to the west of the pier at the Moana Surfrider and turned in a complete circle, filming a Waikiki that was both half civilized and half feral. There were lagoons and brush down to the water's edge, where men and women paraded along in Victorian fashion: The women were covered from ankles to wrists in Victorian dresses, walking alongside men wearing wool suits and skimmers in the middle of summer.

Bonine captured history the way no one remembers it. Common wisdom is that

doing what is now called "The Huntington Hop." Hawaiian surfing in 1900 may have been more dead than alive, but those few who were still surfing were certainly stoked.

When Bonine pointed his kinetograph at the surf of Waikiki, Duke Paoa Kahanamoku was sixteen years old but already well known as a waterman and a beach boy from a family who seemed to have grown up out of the coral. In 1908, Duke and his friends under the *hau* tree at Waikiki formed the *Hui Nalu*, a surfing, swimming, paddling, and canoe-racing club in answer to the *haole* Outrigger Canoe Club that was formed in 1901. As a founding member of *Hui Nalu*, Duke was known for training in the open ocean, swimming past Sans Souci Beach at Waikiki and well out to sea, past the reefs and into shark territory: "I see the sharks all the time," Duke said to anyone concerned. "I don't bother them, and they don't bother me."

Duke's swimming attracted the attention of a *haole* attorney named William T. Rawlins. It was Rawlins who pushed Duke and his friends to form *Hui Nalu*, and now he encouraged Duke to compete in the first Hawaiian Amateur Athletic Union swimming and diving championship, held in August 1911. Competing in murky saltwater in Honolulu Harbor, Duke shook up the world when he tied the world record in the 50-yard freestyle and then shattered the world record for the 100-yard freestyle by 4.6 seconds. There were five certified judges keeping an eye on everything, but the AAU thought there was a fluke or a fraud; some said there were currents in the harbor that rushed him along. Soon after, Duke proved he was no fluke when he easily qualified in Philadelphia for the Olympic team in the 100-meter freestyle,

surfing was all but dead in the Hawaiian Islands at the turn of the century, that the missionary position had swept the water clean of naked surfers and placed them all in suits in front of blackboards. Yet here Bonine films about a dozen surfers in the water at the site that is probably known today as Canoes. They are surfing on old-fashioned *alaia*—yet angling and turning and looking thoroughly modern. One guy is even pumping his board up and down to make it back into the section of a slow-rolling comber,

Tourist Surfer, 1920s
Thanks to the Duke's influence, tourists to Hawai'i were intrigued to try surfing. At least most tourists were. This woman on Waikiki seems dubious about all the fuss—or maybe it's the wool swimsuit "fashions." She stands with a "Mike Jay" board near where the old Outrigger Cane Club once was. Bishop Museum

then broke another world record as he qualified for the 200-meter relay team in New Jersey.

At the 1912 Stockholm Olympics, Duke felt right at home in the pool. At the time, track and field were the big events, and swimming was still a minor Olympic sport. Legend has it that Duke almost missed a preliminary heat when he overslept, but he went on to win gold in the 100-meter freestyle and silver in the 200-meter relay. Duke and fellow American Jim Thorpe were the stars of that Olympics, and they were personally presented their Olympic wreaths and medals by Sweden's King Gustav V.

Duke was suddenly world famous, and his fame brought worldwide attention to the notions of Hawai'i and beach boys and surfing. After the 1912 Olympics,

Duke was invited everywhere to give swimming exhibitions. And more often than not, he traveled with a surfboard at the ready.

Ironically, because of ironclad Olympic rules, Duke was not allowed to work as a beach boy or lifeguard because he was not allowed to be paid to surf or swim in any way. Instead, he built a decent career in Hollywood playing Indian chiefs and shell-laced island natives, but in none of his movies did Duke so much as dip a toe in the water. And he was almost forced to travel because he couldn't really earn a living at home.

Most Hawaiians don't like to leave the Islands and feel homesick when they are halfway around the world, but Duke was not like that. He traveled to the 1920

Wood Belly Board, 3'0"

This 1920s wooden belly board was available for rent on Long Beach, California. Adopted 2002.

Olympics in Antwerp, Belgium, where he won gold medals in the 100-yard freestyle and relay. At the 1924 Olympics, Duke won silver, finishing behind American swimming sensation Johnny Weissmuller, with whom Duke became good friends. In between, Duke was on the move more often than not. His displays of surfing everywhere from Australia to California to Europe made him surfing's global ambassador—and crowned the Duke as the new royalty in the sport of kings.

Even though he was the new king, Duke was still riding on old thrones. From Bonine's film as well as other historical artifacts, the boards being ridden around Waikiki were mostly *alaia*, from 10 feet and shorter. Some *alaia* of the time were as short as 7 feet, 2 to 3 inches thick, flat on top, and with a convex bottom and rounded edges.

The major advances of the time in surfboards came not in design but in materials. The native Hawaiian woods, such as *koa* and *wiliwili*, were being replaced by redwood, pine, and other imported woods. The woods that had originally been used to build boards were in critically short supply, so California redwood was found to be the best substitute. And rather than finishing boards with the time-honored, time-consuming burned *kukui*-nut juice, marine varnish was now the fashion. Throughout the 1920s, these revived *alaia* provided the wings on the waves. *Alaia* boards continued to grow in length by a foot or two, and pointed noses became popular in the mid-1920s. These planks marked the beginning of a transition to modern surfboards, using the ancient *alaia* as a starting point.

Waikiki Redwood Plank, 10'0"

The original owner of this surfboard in the 1920s was Dr. Richard Arnest, who surfed Waikiki in the 1930s. His son cut the shark inlay to make a bar top in the 1950s. Happily, the board was never used as a bar. Adopted 2003

Outrigger Canoe Club Redwood Plank, 11'6"

Shaped in the 1920s, this solid redwood board was used by Waikiki Beach's Outrigger Canoe Club members from the 1920s through the 1940s. Eventually the board spent some years at the beach entrance as a decorative totem before being removed when the club was relocated. Uncle Dave Nuuhiwa remembered the famous board and its story. Previously owned by Joe Alphabet. Adopted 2002.

George Freeth: Hotdogger and Surfboard Hot Rodder

Most of the Waikiki beach boys were pure Hawaiian, but George Freeth was of mixed ancestry. Born in 1883 of Hawaiian and Irish parentage, by 1900 Freeth was standing up and riding waves on a heavy, 16-foot *olo*.

During the first years of the twentieth century, Freeth came into his prime as a water athlete. A member of the Diamond Head Athletic Club, the Healani swim team, and later the Honolulu Swim Club, he actively competed starting in 1906. Freeth was also a star surfer, and on July 3, 1907, the *Honolulu Star* labeled him "the most expert surfboard rider in the world." The newspaper went on to explain: "Some years ago (surfing) had become almost unknown, except by tradition, when Freeth, who is one of the most expert and graceful swimmers and divers in the Territory, took up the sport and by diligent and intelligent practice developed until he is now probably as accomplished as any of the ancient wave-riders." The *Honolulu Star* also noted that Freeth could ride a board while standing on his head or his hands. As surfing historian Joel T. Smith stated, he was perhaps the first hotdogger.

But more important, the newspaper reported that Freeth experimented with his surfboard's design. In another feature on Freeth on July 3, 1907, the *Pacific Commercial Advertiser* wrote, "Freeth tried a number of surf boards, some long and narrow, others shorter but with more breadth, and also of varying thicknesses. Finally, he found the one which was suited to him." Freeth was experimenting with surfboard design at a time when building boards was a lost art. The *koa* and *wiliwili* woods that traditionally were used to construct surfboards were hard to come by, so most of the boards were made from imported California redwood.

By 1907, Freeth was one of several young Hawaiians at the vanguard of resurrecting surfing.

George Freeth, 1915
Freeth spent much of his life in Hawai'i surfing and hot-rodding his surfboards. He's pictured here in Redondo Beach, California, where he came by invitation from Henry Huntington, helping to promote surfing along the way.

Among his crew of beach boys were the Kahanamoku brothers, Edward "Dudie" Miller, George "Dad" Center, and others.

CHAPTER 2

The Thoroughly Modern *Olo*

Kookboxes, Redwood Swastikas, and Balsa Flyers

THE ROARING TWENTIES AND THE SOARING THIRTIES

Surfing Heroes, 1920s
Tom Blake and Duke Kahanamoku pose with one of Blake's hollow paddleboards on a Hawaiian beach.
Surfing Heritage Foundation

Opposite:
Tom Blake
Catalina, 11'8"
Blake innovated his hollow surfboards as an improvement over the solid redwood boards used in Hawai'i. This original 1930s example still retains its original drainage plug and the painted "Catalina" label. Due to the fragile nature of the plywood construction, most of the Blake hollow boards are now long gone. Adopted 1997.

Just as Hawai'i divides its history into Before Cook and After Cook, so does Duke Kahanamoku divide his life into Before Olympics and After Olympics. In the same way, Tom Blake divides his life into Before Duke and After Duke, and now surfers divide the history of the surfboard into Before Blake and After Blake.

In 1920, Duke Kahanamoku was returning from the Olympic Games in Belgium where he won another gold medal. Crossing the United States on his way home to Hawai'i, Duke was one of a group of swimmers who went to a theater in Detroit to watch a newsreel on the Olympics.

At the theater that night was a young man from Wisconsin named Tom Blake who was just starting to make a name for himself in the water. Blake remembered the evening well, as he was quoted in *Tom Blake: The Uncommon Journey of a Pioneer Waterman* by Gary Lynch: "A motion picture newsreel showing the United States swimming team's performance at Antwerp was running at a local theater. Duke and his fellow Hawaiian teammates came to see themselves in action on the screen.

I, too, had come to see the film and I was so impressed when I found myself near this champion that I intercepted him in the theater lobby and asked to shake his hand. 'Sure!' Duke replied, smiling and eager to please, as always. He held out to me his big, soft paw of a hand and gave me a firm, hearty handshake. It made a lasting impression. I felt that somehow he had included an invitation to me to come over to his own Hawaiian Islands."

In Olympian terms, what Duke did when he shook Blake's hand was pass on a baton of surf stoke. The young man from Wisconsin would become one of the pioneers of the surfing lifestyle, propounding to everyone everywhere how to live clean, live simple, and live well. But above all, Tom Blake would take old Hawaiian ideas to create new Hawaiian ideas and have a profound effect on surfboard design, one that still resonates today.

The King of the Kookbox

Before Blake became a surfer, he was a young man from a broken home, wandering and trying to find himself. Blake was born in 1902 to loving parents. His mother died of tuberculosis when he was eleven months old, and for the first sixteen years of his life, he was raised by relatives. Blake had athleticism in his genes, and while he tried football and other land sports, he excelled in the water. When the local lakes in Wisconsin weren't frozen over, Blake swam. Like a lot of young men who would become great surfers, Blake turned to the water to bathe a lonely soul in those liqueurs that come from hard work and exhaustion in the waves.

Blake never finished school, as his high school closed due to an influenza outbreak. He began a life of wandering that

Solid Cedar Waikiki Board, 10'0"
The cedar boards making up this surfboard were brought to Hawai'i in 1925 and the board was hand-shaped on the beach in Waikiki. With the introduction of lighter hollow boards, this board was discarded. Left under a tree in Manoa Valley, it sat unwanted for the next sixty years. Adopted 2001.

Folklore

Hawaiian school children look up in awe at the giant surfboards of their ancestry. Blake was responsible for digging these boards out of the Bishop Museum's vast holdings and restoring them. Bishop Museum

landed him in California in September 1921. Needing a place to work and train, Blake first snuck into the Los Angeles Athletic Club. Here, he earned a berth on the team by competing against and waxing the national swimming champion, Walter Spence. After that, coach Fred Cady took

Blake under his wing and ushered him to competitions around the country. Blake excelled at all distances, from the 220 to the mile.

Tom Blake was 20 in 1921 when he first tried surfing. He borrowed a large, heavy redwood plank from surfer Haig

Tom Blake's Quiver, 1930

Blake showed off what a thoroughly modern quiver looked like in 1930. At a sturdy six feet, Blake was dwarfed by all of these boards, the shortest being an 11' redwood "riding board" that was 23" wide and 3¹/₂" thick. Next to that was a 12-footer made of red cedar that Blake used both for surfing and paddling. The third board in the quiver was one of the hollow olo Blake made from boards he had seen in the Bishop Museum. This board was 14'6" long and 20" wide and weighed 120 pounds. The fourth board was Okohola, the riding version of his hollow olo-inspired shapes originally made for paddle racing. The last two boards in the quiver are the two that caused all the fuss. They were identical, hollow 16-footers, the one with the Outrigger Canoe Club logo on the deck was a lighter version used for racing, while the sixth board was identical but heavier and used for training. These were the boards Blake used to break records in the Ala Wai Canal, sparking a battle—and changing the surfboards everyone rode for the next eighty years.
Surfing Heritage Foundation

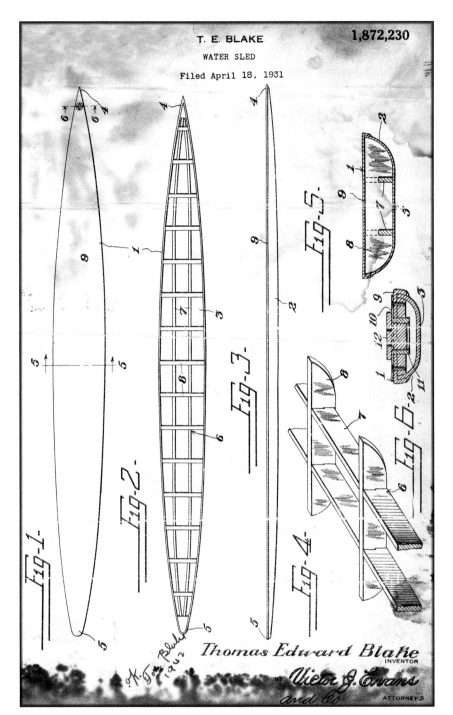

T. E. BLAKE

WATER SLED

Filed April 18, 1931

1,872,230

Thomas Edward Blake
INVENTOR

Tom Blake Hollow Board Patent, 1931

Tom Blake filed for a patent on his hollow-board construction, seen here on his "water sled." Surfing Heritage Foundation

Tom Blake Logo, 1930s

Priest out of Peterson's boathouse at the Crystal Pier in Santa Monica and took it to the Canyon Break in north Santa Monica: "Took it out, tried to ride it," Blake wrote about the experience in his 1935 book *Hawaiian Surfboard.* "Caught a wave, took a big, mean, nasty pearl dive in a three-foot wave. Got shook up, put the board away and forgot about it for a while." A long while.

Over the next three years, Blake won success as a swimmer and jump-started a Hollywood career as a stuntman. Then, while working as a Santa Monica lifeguard in 1924, he found an unloved 9-foot 10-inch redwood plank at the Santa Monica Swimming Club. He surfed the board at Santa Monica Canyon and gagged again. But two days later, he got a good ride. The hook was set.

The lingering power of Duke's hand-shake finally pulled Blake to Hawai'i in 1924. What he found was close to heaven.

Waikiki was lined with a couple of resort hotels, but it was mostly still wild. Men and women were riding the waves in fast-moving outrigger canoes and on surfboards, mostly *alaia* and some *olo*, the longest, heaviest boards used by the beach boys to teach surfing to tourists and ride tandem with women. When the time was theirs, the beach boys were hot-dogging it on finless hardwood boards.

Blake came to Hawai'i with the beater board he rescued in California, but knew once he arrived that he needed something better. His first Hawaiian board was a narrow-tail, 10-foot-plus redwood bought for just $25 from a local surfer named Edric Cooke. At the time, Blake posed proudly with the board as if it were a favored girlfriend and still spoke fondly about it many years later: "I probably surfed that for a year or so and found it to be a good board,"

Blake said in an interview with Gary Lynch in April of 1989, "but that was before fins and it was a little squirrely on a wave. But it was a good board, light and easy to catch a wave with."

In Hawai'i, Blake's water skills and reputation threw him in with the beach boys and the Kahanamoku brothers. Duke wasn't around for Blake's first visit, but his legend was everywhere. Duke's brother Sam was also an Olympic-quality swimmer and he toured Blake around, let him ride one of Duke's boards, took him out tandem into the Waikiki surf, and showed him some of that undiluted *aloha* for which Hawai'i was then famous. "From those days onward I was fascinated by surfing," Blake wrote in an article called "Duke, As I Knew Him" for *Paradise of the Pacific* magazine in 1931. "With this came an ever-growing interest in the design and

Tom Blake Boards Brochure, 1930s
Surfing Heritage Foundation

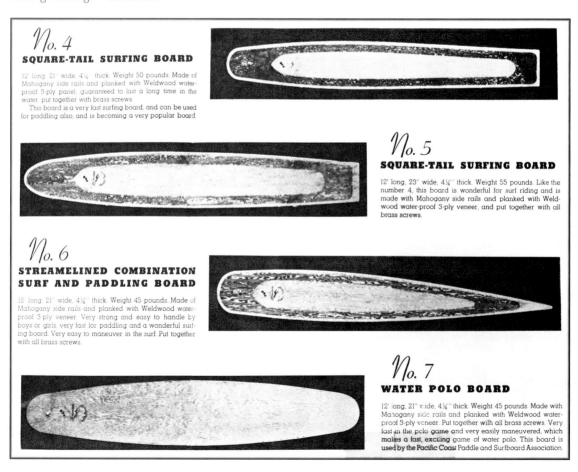

Hollowed Redwood Paddleboard, 14'6"

This hollowed-out solid-redwood racing paddleboard was constructed in the 1930s. It was purchased at a police auction by Harvey Toda, who used the board for competition before passing it on to his son. This board is extremely narrow and made from a solid slab of redwood. The body was hollowed out and decking applied to cut down on weight. The board was later partly eaten away by termites. Unrestored, it retains its original brass drain plug. Adopted 2005.

Joseph "Scooter Boy" Kaouiki Hollow Paddleboard, 12'0"

This spruce and mahogany hollow board was built in the late 1930s by the Funai boatbuilders. The Funai were Japanese craftsmen based in Hawai'i who built the akule, ahi, and aku sampans of the fishing fleet before World War II. They also moonlighted, building surfboards for the Waikiki Beach boys. This board was owned by old-time Waikiki surfer Joseph "Scooter Boy" Kaouiki. Scooter Boy was an icon in Waikiki, as he was regularly in the water with his poi dog, Sandy, whom he taught to surf with him. Scooter Boy was one of the few surfers of that era who could surf these large skegless paddleboards, doing radical maneuvers and turns in the surf off Waikiki. This board was oil-sealed, and all screws were covered with wooden plugs. The brass-chrome handle on the tail is original. Adopted 2005.

building of surfboards which might make possible greater rides. I went to the Bishop Museum in Honolulu and there began to study the enormous old boards preserved from the days of the ancient Hawaiians, who had been master surf-riders long before the influence of foreign nations took over the life of the Islands. Among these were the long, narrow, giants of the kind called *olo* boards by the natives."

Blake's first trip to Hawai'i lasted less than a year, and he returned to California with visions of hula girls and *olo* dancing in his head. He worked as a lifeguard again at the Santa Monica Swimming Club, where he was jazzed to find himself swimming alongside Duke, who had taken a job lifeguarding with the Santa Monica Beach Club. Duke and Blake became fast friends, working and surfing together, both of them most likely homesick for Hawai'i.

In September 1926, Blake picked up another Los Angeles waterman named Sam Reid and they drove together out into the sticks of the Malibu Rancho. At the time, the Rindge family was losing its battle with the state of California to keep its vast rancho private, but the property was still fenced and patrolled by cowboys

with guns: "We took our 10-foot red-woods out of the Essex rumble seat and paddled the mile to a beautiful, white crescent-shaped beach that didn't have a footprint on it," Reid remembered in a 1994 Santa Monica Heritage Museum exhibit called *Cowabunga!*, "There was no audience but the seagulls."

Blake wasn't as impressed by Malibu's surf as Reid was. It was only 3 feet, and they were riding redwood boards that were around 10 feet tall and 22 inches wide and probably made for Santa Monica beach break surf and not those long, green Malibu walls. But that first session opened a spot that would have a profound influence on surfboard design, as surfers to come in the 1940s and 1950s hot-rodded their boards to do justice to that perfect little wave.

By 1926, Blake established a migratory pattern that generations of surfers have followed since: California in the summer for work, Hawai'i in the winter for play. After that Malibu session in September 1926, Blake went to Hawai'i for his third trip, and this time he stayed awhile. He also sparked a revolution that would take surfboard design away from hardwood planks and into new materials, designs, and directions.

Birth of the Hollow Boards

Blake returned to the Bishop Museum with a renewed interest in the ancient Hawaiian boards stored there. There were three boards in particular that grabbed his attention: "Strange as it may seem," Blake wrote in "Surf Riding—The Ancient and Royal Sport" in *Pan Pacific Magazine* in 1931, "three old-style Hawaiian surf-boards of huge dimensions and weight have hung on the walls of the Bishop

Paddleboard, 12'7"
Built in the 1930s out of mahogany, this kookbox was later adapted to house a glass undersea viewing box. The brass drain hole is original. Adopted 1999.

Aquaglider #1, 9'4"

During the 1930s era of the wooden kookbox paddleboards like Tom Blake's Catalina, the Aquaglider was designed and built by a Mr. Taylor; no other information is known about the man or company. Much lighter than the plywood and redwood hollow boards, the Aquaglider was made of channeled tin on the bottom. The upper side deck was a solid plywood piece riveted to the tin bottom. This board originally belonged to Gerhart "G" Stangeland, who worked on the construction of the Dance Hall at the Long Beach Pier in the early 1900s. The board later passed to his son, Gary "The Goose" Stangeland. His nephew Mike got the board from Gary in exchange for a fireman's badge. Adopted 2005.

Museum in Honolulu for twenty years or more without anyone doing more than wonder how in the world these great boards were used, and were they not too long and heavy to be practicable. Two fine examples of a now extinct design are these two old boards on which Chief Paki once rode the Kalahuewehe [sic] surf at Waikiki."

Blake saw a greatness in these boards that the museum curators did not, and he began a campaign to restore the boards to their greatness and display them with dignity: "I had the privilege, and hard work, of restoring Paki's museum boards to their original condition," Blake wrote in *Hawaiian Surfriders* in 1935. "For twenty years or more they had been hanging or tied with wire against the stone wall on the outside of the museum, covered with some old reddish paint and rather neglected. My inquiries into the art of surfriding disclosed to me the true value of these two old *koa* boards. They are the only two ancient surfboards of authentic *olo* design known to be in existence today. In the restoration of Paki's old boards, I discovered that they are undoubtedly much older than anyone suspected. In fact, they were probably already antiques when Paki acquired them."

**Surfing Tandem,
1930s**

*Tom Blake and Mary
Ann Hawkins ride in
tandem on a Hawaiian
wave.* Doc Ball

Inspired by the elbow grease he invested taking those *olo* down to their original skin, Blake began making modern *olo*, but they weren't for surfing as much as they were for paddling races. Blake's goal was to significantly lighten surfboards and paddleboards, and the first step he took was drilling holes in one of his custom *olo*. Blake took a piece of redwood that was 16 feet long, 2 feet wide, and 4 inches thick. He drilled holes in the board from top to bottom, let the board dry and cure for a month, then covered the board top and bottom with a thin veneer to seal the holes.

The result was a board that was 15 feet long, 19 inches wide, 4 inches thick, and 110 pounds. Blake was quoted by Leonard Lueras in his 1984 *Surfing, the Ultimate Pleasure*, stating that he "drilled it full of holes to lighten and dry it out, then plugged them up. Result: accidental invention of the first hollow surf-board."

On August 5, 1928, he unveiled his new secret weapon at the First Pacific Coast Surfriding Championships, a contest he helped organize and the first wave-riding competition contest of any kind on the mainland. "When I appeared with it for the first time before 10,000 people gathered for a holiday and to watch the races, it was regarded as silly," Blake recalled. "Handling this heavy board alone, I got off to a poor start, the rest of the field gaining a 30-yard lead in the meantime. It really looked bad for the board and my reputation and hundreds openly laughed. But a few minutes later it turned to applause because the big board led the way to the finish of the 880-yard course by fully 100 yards."

Blake refined the hollow-board concept in 1929 by making boards of carved chambers, with a veneer on both sides. These boards weren't a solid slab of hardwood poked full of holes. Instead, they were made like an airplane wing, and they flew—with controversy streaming out behind like a jet contrail. In *Hawaiian Surfriders 1935*, Blake wrote about this next phase in design, which was inspired by the Hawaiian people, but also Cook's people: "In the later part of 1929, after three years of experimenting, I introduced at Waikiki a new type of surfboard . . . In reality the design was taken from the ancient Hawaiian type of board, also from the English racing shell. It was called a 'cigar board,' because a newspaper reporter thought it was shaped like a giant cigar. This board was really graceful and beautiful to look at, and in performance so good that officials of the annual surfboard paddling championship immediately had a set of nine of them built for use during the 1930 Hawaiian Paddling Championship races."

While Blake designed these hollowed *olo* to wax *okole* in paddleboard races, he also built them for surfing. In December 1929, he created *Okohola*, a hollow *olo* designed for riding waves. These boards were made from redwood and featured a

Surf Shop Sign Hollow Paddleboard, 9'0"
After many years of use, this classic kookbox was resurrected as a surfshop sign along the West Coast. Adopted 2005.

Tom Blake, 1939
The picture of the fitness and health he proscribed, Blake surfs Palos Verdes Estates with obvious stoke.
Doc Ball

flat deck. Excellent for paddling, they were also great in rolling Waikiki surf. Catching a wave out beyond the break, Blake could slide the *Okohola* sweetly with the gentle slope of the breakers.

On December 1, 1929, Blake unveiled his new paddleboard to the crowds that lined the Ala Wai Canal for the first in a series of midwinter paddleboard races. This race attracted a lot of attention and competitors, and they brought a wide range of boards. Blake shaved five seconds off the 100-yard record, and started a bit of *hu hu.* Some felt Blake had an unfair advantage on his light, hollow "cigar" design because all of the boards in the paddleboard race

were designed to be surfed. Blake's board was built specifically to be paddled, and his victory in that event started grumbling that would continue for many years.

The big event of the year was the Hawaiian Surfboard Paddling Championship held in the Ala Wai Canal on New Year's Day 1930. While officials ordered nine of Blake's new *olo*-inspired hollow paddleboards for the event, defending

Redwood Laminated Plank, 11'6"
This 1930s board is one of the earliest known examples of a lighter-weight plank, made using chambered laminated construction. Late in its life, the board was used as a bartop (see the screwholes in the bottom). It was eventually returned to its proper use. Adopted 2001.

champion Tommy Keakona protested the race due to Blake's board and refused to compete. Something new was in the air because of the "cigar" boards, and 3,000 people lined the canal to watch. Paddling for the Outrigger Canoe Club against the Hui Nalu and Queen's Surfers, Blake won the half-mile Men's Open, shaving 2:13 off the old record. In the feature event of the day, he beat the record for the 100-yard open by 5 seconds. He was declared the star of the meet and his cigar board was a hit. But not with everyone. Some called Blake's creations "kookboxes" for their kooky handling—a kind moniker in comparison to other names. And many traditional watermen felt Blake's wins were hollow victories.

The surfing versions of Blake's hollow boards also opened up new places to surf. The small *alaia* in fashion along Waikiki didn't have a prayer of catching the biggest bluebirds that broke on the biggest south-swell days. But that changed with the modern *olo*. It was in August 1930 that Blake had his "longest ride on a surfboard," when he caught a wave at first break Ka-lehua-wehe and rode it to the beach, equaling and possibly surpassing Duke's famous ride of 1917. The break Blake refers to is now known as Outside Cunha: "Today Ka-lehua-wehe surf is coming into vogue again," Blake wrote in *Hawaiian Surfriders, 1935*. "It breaks only when big swells are running but is the aristocrat of all surfs. However, as yet, not 10 per cent of the surfriders are familiar with its hazardous, thrilling rides. The fact that the old Hawaiian chiefs gathered at the beach to ride it sets their standard of sportsmanship up. The prevailing custom of using short or ten foot long boards until 1930 had much to do with not riding this

surf. It is a mile paddle from the Outrigger Club and with a short board the rider has to get dangerously near the break to catch these big waves, with the result [that] when one mentioned going to Ka-lehua-wehe surf excuses come thick and fast. However, my new hollow board makes the paddle out there simple and the swells can be easily picked up, just as the ancients could do with their *olo* boards of *wiliwili* and *koa*. So those who have hollow boards are taking to the big Kalahuewehe surf more and more each year and eventually will have the sport of big wave riding as popular as in olden days."

It was the midst of the Great Depression and millions were unemployed. Yet Blake was living simply in a shack near Diamond Head, spending his days enjoying some of the best things in life that are free—the ocean and sun and wind and waves. In April 1931, he applied for a patent for his "Water Sled" hollow board, and the patent was granted in August 1932. This allowed Blake to license his designs to manufacturers, beginning a run through the 1930s of agreements with the Thomas Rogers Company, Robert Mitchell Manufacturing Company, Los Angeles Ladder Company, and the Catalina Equipment Company to turn Blake's concepts into surfboards, paddleboards, and lifesaving boards.

A 1934 Thomas Rogers brochure displayed seven kinds of Blake-designed hollow boards: The Paddle Board was made of Philippine Mahogany and came 14 feet long and 55 pounds for men, 12 feet long and 50 pounds for women, and 10 feet long and 40 pounds for children.

The Streamlined Life Guard Board was also made of Philippine Mahogany and was 14 feet long, weighing 85 pounds.

Hollow-Board Revelation and Revolution

The *Honolulu Star-Bulletin* featured an assessment of Tom Blake's hollow-board design in an article from September 28, 1934: "Tom Blake, surfboard expert of Waikiki beach, has just returned from a year's tour of the mainland introducing his development, the new Hollow Surfboard, to the public on the mainland United States for lifeguard work, surfriding, paddling and aqua-planing purposes.

"Blake holds the U.S. patent on the Hollow Surfboard and has been fortunate in interesting eastern capital and a large Cincinnati, Ohio, manufacturing concern in the making and distribution of his board.

"A very enthusiastic reception of the Hollow Hawaiian Surfboard in the States is reported. Important life guard services throughout the country have adopted the Hollow Surfboard as standard equipment for rescue work, and, of course, life guards are becoming good surfers.

"Extensive surfriding is already to be seen in Southern California and from Florida to Maine on the Atlantic coast.

"The American Red Cross officials believe that the Hollow Surfboard is the greatest piece of life saving equipment ever developed and are giving him great help and support in his work, the inventor states.

"In the new 1934 design, Mr. Blake feels he has at last produced an excellent riding board. It is short, broad, and buoyant; very easy to catch a wave with and paddle fast. When standing it goes into a slide or out with the slightest pressure of the feet.

"The board is made of genuine African mahogany, the equivalent of Hawaiian *koa* wood. The Robert Mitchell Mfg. Co., of Cincinnati, Ohio, are the exclusive manufacturers of the invention."

This board was used by the American Red Cross and also recommended for tandem surfing.

The Beach Boy Square-Tail Board was 12 feet long, weighed 80 pounds, and was made of solid mahogany fastened with all brass screws. The brochure copy claimed: "This board is wonderful for surf riding and is a good tandem board, it is used a lot in the Hawaiian Islands and a board that will carry weight perfectly. There are a great number of this style boards now being used on the Pacific Coast."

It had only been ten years since Duke had shaken the hand of an eager young man in Detroit, but now Blake was thanking Duke and the Hawaiian people by taking designs from their ancestors and passing them on to their offspring.

The Pacific System Homes Swastika

Tom Blake was not the only young Californian to travel to Hawai'i and get infected by the surfing bug. As the 1920s roared, one Meyers Butte caught a wave, sat on top of the world, and went back to California with his head spinning.

Butte was the son of William Butte, a founding partner in 1908 of Pacific System Ready Cut Homes. By the 1920s, the firm was on its way to becoming the largest home builder in the world. Located in Los Angeles, its operation covered 25 acres and was self-contained with a

Pacific System Homes Swastika, 10'1"

Greg Noll shaped this modern-day rendition of one of the first boards to be produced by a surfboard factory. Pacific System Homes' first boards carried the Swastika logo, a 2,000-year-old symbol of good fortune that was only later adopted by the Nazis. Few original Swastika boards survive today. Noll created this replica using the original blueprints and the same types of materials—balsa and redwood. Adopted 2001.

Look
for the
Swastika
emblem
on
every
Board

WAIKIKI SURF-BOARD CO.
a subsidiary of
PACIFIC *System* **HOMES** INC.
America's Largest Home Builders—30 Years of Leadership
Factory and Office
5800 SOUTH BOYLE AVE.   LOS ANGELES, CALIF.

Swastika and Waikiki Logos

steam powerplant, lumberyard, machine shops, art studio, and architecture department. And of course, there was an abundance of large-capacity wood-production machinery like planers, routers, profiling saws, and hydraulic lamination presses, all ideal for building surfboards.

When the stock market crashed in October 1929, Meyers Butte was at Stanford, training for an Olympic berth as a wrestler. The Depression instead forced him to come home and get involved with the family business. Butte realized there was no company providing quality hardwood surfboards to an ever-growing market, and saw his father's company perfectly situated and set up to fill the gap. Butte switched a small section of Pacific Ready Cut System Homes to surfboard production. The big breakthrough came when he and his associates found a waterproof glue that would hold together in the wear and tear of sun and saltwater.

Butte's first boards were similar in style and shape to the basic surfboards in use at Waikiki. These early boards were constructed of solid redwood with long lag bolts holding them together. Later, the redwood boards were routed out and featured dowel-and-biscuit joinery. Contrasting colored pine strips were incorporated into some of the redwood decks. Later models had alternating narrow strips of dark- and light-colored woods. As demand grew, the company moved into using balsa for the bulk of the boards, with redwood rails and mahogany plywood decks.

During the course of its years manufacturing boards, Pacific System Homes employed a number of well-known surfers, including Pete Peterson and Lorrin "Whitey" Harrison: "When I came back from Hawaii with my first wife, we lived in Dana Point," Whitey was quoted on www.legendarysurfers.com. "I started fishing commercial, and then I got a motorcycle and rode it all the way to Los Angeles to work at Pacific Redi-cut Systems Homes for a summer. Tulie Clark and Carroll 'Laholio' Bertolet worked there too. Quite

Waikiki Tourist, 1930s

The Pacific System Homes board may have just been a photo prop to show off in snapshots to friends back home. Yet many a tourist was hooked on wave-riding after boarding a Swastika and sitting on top of the world. Voyageur Press Archives

Swastika Brochure, 1930s

Pacific System Homes published this early blue brochure for its Swastika line of boards.
Surfing Heritage Foundation

a few surfers worked there, this was about 1931. We were shipping sixty boards a month to Hawaii. . . . There was this guy there named 'Dutch' that was notching these swastika symbols in some of the boards, and he couldn't speak a word of English. They called these 'Swastika boards.' He'd mix glue and we'd glue up the blanks. Then we'd run them through a shaper to get a rough shape then finish them with hard planes and sandpaper. It drove me crazy, but it was work. They sold a balsa redwood plank for about $25. The rail shape was full with a square upper edge and rounded lower edge. The typical board was 10 feet long, 23 inches wide,

A Riot of Fun for Water Enthusiasts

with

SWASTIKA

HAWAIIAN SURF-BOARDS — PADDLE-BOARDS
AQUA-PLANES

No instruction is necessary to ride a Swastika. You "get the knack" on your first ride and each succeeding glide shoreward will bring thrill after thrill. Three Swastika products are available to aquatists—Surf Boards, Aqua-planes and Paddle-boards. More Swastika surf-boards are used at Waikiki than any other professional type—made in Los Angeles and shipped to Hawaii. They are preferred exclusively by the most spectacular riders at Honolulu, including the renowned Duke Kahanamoku. In Southern California the foremost movie stars, club men and athletes vouch for the Swastika. These are positively the fleetest and most beautiful of surf-boards.

Genuine Hawaiian Surf-Boards

Swastika Surf-boards are made of solid Balsa wood. They have Redwood band strips and a Redwood nose and tail piece, affording protection against contact. A 10-foot surf-board weighs only 45 pounds because it is made principally of Balsa wood weighing 20% lighter than cork. All parts are doweled, assuring maximum rigidity and durability. Stocked in 10 and 11-foot lengths. Special designs and lengths made to order. We also manufacture 5 and 6-foot surf-boards (curved-up nose type) especially popular with juveniles. Finished in natural colors visible for great distances.

Perfectly-balanced Aqua-Planes

Swastika Aqua-planes are designed to maintain proper balance. When towed behind speed boats they offer fascinating thrills. Equipped with rope and rubber mat. Colorful, durable—easy to operate by a novice. May be used as free tow-boards.

High-Speed Paddle-Boards

Swastika paddle-boards are stocked in 12 and 14-ft. lengths. The latter has a buoyancy of 450 pounds. These are extensively used by life guards for life saving, but are equally popular with swimmers for lounging out beyond the breakers. With a Swastika Paddle-board one can skim over the water three or four times as fast as straight swimming. It's a great aid for developing the arms, neck and shoulders.

Incomparable Workmanship

Swastikas are built for a life-time of service under the personal direction of a professional surf-board aquatist in the largest house-building plant on the Pacific Coast. The woods are specially selected. The Balsa wood is selected from finest imported stocks, scientifically kilned, laminated and cabinet-finished by expert craftsmen. All Swastikas are guaranteed against defects for one year.

How to Order

If your local sporting goods house does not carry Swastikas in stock you may order direct from the manufacturer. Immediate shipment. State size desired, route of shipment.

Exclusive Manufact...

SWASTIKA SURF-...

A subsidiary o...

PACIFIC SYSTEM...

Factory and ...
5800 South Boyle Avenue, ...

MYERS P. BUTTE

Phone JEfferson 2261

SWASTIKA SURF-BOARD CO.

Manufacturers

SWASTIKA

Hawaiian Surf-Boards ⊕ *Aqua-Planes, Paddle Boards*

5800 South Boyle Ave.,
Los Angeles, California

Gentlemen:

We manufacture and carry in stock a complete line of surf boards, paddle boards and aqua planes. For the past six years we have been manufacturing Hawaiian surf boards and shipping them to Honolulu, where they are known as the "Genuine Hawaiian Surf Board". Our merchandise is sold in Honolulu, Florida and New York, as well as California. Our line is an entirely new type of surf board and paddle board, which are made principally of Balsa Wood, which is 25% lighter than cork. Our merchandise has new, scientifically designed stream lines which appreciably increase the speed. A complete list of our merchandise is as follows:

5 ft. Surf Board, curved up nose, made of redwood and sugar pine, finished in natural or painted colors, Your cost $2.25 ea.

6 ft. Surf Board, curved up nose, made of redwood and sugar pine, finished in natural or painted colors, Your cost $2.35 ea.

10 ft. Hawaiian surf board, made of balsa wood, laminated and banded with redwood, 4 inches thick, approximate weight 45 lbs. finished in natural wood, ... Your cost $27.00 ea.

11 ft. Hawaiian surf board, same as above, only approximate weight 50 lbs. . . . . Your cost $29.00 ea.

12 ft. Hawaiian surf board, same as above, only approximate weight 55 lbs. . . . . Your cost $31.00 ea.

16 ft. Paddle Board, made of balsa wood, laminated and banded with redwood, 3 in. thick, approximate weight 35 pounds, ... Your cost $21.50 ea.

Swastika
Brochure, 1930s
Surfing Heritage Foundation

"I believe surf-board riding is one of the greatest sports and best exercises known. It has enabled me to keep in good physical condition. I look forward to the joy and thrill of sliding down the waves on my Swastika Surf Board."

George Dyna

"I have found much enjoyment in riding my Swastika Hawaiian Surf Board. This board has proved to be perfectly balanced, light and sturdy."

Geo. "Typhoon" Spencer

SWASTIKA
Hawaiian Surf Board
and Aqua Planes

Riding the billowy breakers at dashing speeds on a Swastika Hawaiian Surf Board is a thrilling sport without rival. The buoyancy and lightness of Swastikas make them extremely agile and full of life. Zipping along on the crest of a breaker, just in front of the foaming caps, is the greatest of all aqua sports. Swastikas are finished in bright colors and can be seen for great distances along the beach. Racing with Swastika Boards is the reigning sport on the Pacific Coast. Learning to ride is a simple task. After experiencing just one thrilling shore-ward dash, no day at the beach is complete without a Swastika. The only rival of the Swastika Surf Board for sheer thrill is the Swastika Aqua Plane. It is constructed to afford safety and a smooth even glide. Lightness and buoyancy, combined with proper location of tow-line, prevents the board from diving out from under the rider. These Aqua-Planes are equipped with a free towing device which provides additional sport and thrill. All Swastikas are guaranteed for one year against defects. They are made from selected, properly-kilned woods, by expert craftsmen. These Hawaiian Surf Boards are laminated and have four air chambers throughout. Dowelling of all parts assures extreme rigidness and durability. Special salt-resistant application assures a durable finish and long life to the board.

"The Swastika Hawaiian Surf Board has surpassed all my expectations. In the past four years I have continually ridden these boards and believe that the present design is the last word in surf boards."

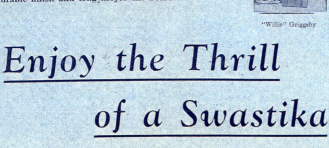

Enjoy the Thrill
of a Swastika

"Willie" Griggsby

Swastika Brochure, 1930s
Surfing Heritage Foundation

and 22 inches across the tail block. They also made and sold paddleboards. They had me racing them against all the other boards up and down the coast. They would cut all the balsa scrap into blocks, glue them together and cut them into a plan shape. Then we'd cover the top and bottom with $1/8$-inch mahogany sheets and then laminate redwood strips along the sides which ended with redwood noses and tail blocks. They worked pretty

good, and they were light!"

From early on, Pacific System Homes surfboards featured a swastika symbol on the nose; the brand was later moved to the tail. There are several stories about the origin of the Swastika model name. In the early 1930s, the ancient symbol still represented health and good fortune; it is found in cultures, continents, and eras from ancient Greece to India. The word *swastika* is Sanskrit, translating as "the

Lorrin "Whitey" Harrison Kookbox, 13'6"

This redwood board was shaped by Whitey Harrison at the Pacific System Homes factory in the 1930s and autographed. Adopted 2001.

Swastika Brochure, 1930s
Surfing Heritage Foundation

**Swastika and
Waikiki Logos**

welfare-bringing thing," and that was how the Buttes intended it. But with the arrival of the Nazis in Germany and the coming of World War II, the swastika took on new meaning. Wilson Butte, Meyers' son, said to Craig Stecyk in *The Surfer's Journal*, "My father abandoned it to avoid any controversy soon after Hitler began using it. The Waikiki boards came out around 1938."

In the surfing version of carrying coals to Newcastle, Meyers Butte shipped six Swastika boards to Hawai'i in 1932. Far

from getting laughed off the beach, the Swastikas became objects of desire: "The Swastika boards were droolers," Dale Velzy was quoted in Craig Stecyk's article. "Everybody had home-mades or hand-me-downs, so people really wanted a Pacific System. There were a lot of them around places where rich guys who had gotten them in Hawaii hung out, like the Bel Air Bay Club, the Jonathon Club, the Balboa Bay Club and the Santa Monica Swim Club."

Still, the hollow boards of Blake and Pacific System Homes became only a branch of the family tree of surfboard design, not the trunk from which all other designs stemmed from afterward. Blake went

Pacific System Homes, 10'0"

Pacific System Homes constructed and sold the world's first mass-produced surfboards, starting in the 1930s. This is an original, never-restored board made of balsa and redwood. The plank shape is typical of the late 1930s and early 1940s. Pacific System Homes boards were tremendously popular, and came in diverse shapes and lengths. Adopted 1996.

on to produce plastic boards in the 1950s, yet his *olo*-inspired hollow boards were a dead end in surfing. These mammoth hollow boards ruled on Hawaiian and even some Californian beaches for years, but meanwhile the surfboard's evolution took off from earlier solid, wide-tailed designs.

Taking Wing on Balsa Boards

In 1926, Hawaiian surfer Lorrin Thurston appeared on Waikiki one day with what looked like a typical surfboard. Yet when he hefted it up easily in his arms, the other surfers knew this wasn't their usual 100-pound redwood hardwood board nor even a 55-pound hollow board. Thurston had found a new, lighter wood, imported to Hawai'i by the *haole* from Asia and South America. Known as balsa, it would make surfboards not only lighter, but correspondingly faster and more maneuverable. As Duke Kahanamoku wrote: "To Thurston … goes the credit of introducing the balsa wood board in 1926. It was really a revival of the *wili wili* boards used by the old Hawaiian chiefs."

Francis Preston "Pete" Peterson was another early surfer to ride balsa. Born in Galveston, Texas, in 1913, he was brought up under rigid Scandinavian ideals of right and wrong. The tremendous Galveston hurricane of 1919 didn't kill his family, but it did destroy their livelihood, forcing them west to California. By January 1920, the family was operating the Crystal Beach Bathhouse in Santa Monica, a focal point of

Beach Boys, 1937
Surfers were hired as extras for the 1937 film Waikiki Wedding, *and posed here at Nanakuli Beach, Oahu, in front of their boards. From left: Curley Cornwell, "Ox" Keaulana, unidentified, Dave "Panama" Baptiste, four unidentified, and Freddy Wilhelm.* Photograph by N. R. Farbman, Bishop Museum

the beach for moviemakers and watermen like Duke Kahanamoku and Tom Blake. "Among the many customers at the bathhouse was a group of Hawaiians, some of the first to come to this country," Peterson was quoted in an article by Craig Lockwood in *The Surfer's Journal.* "[I] became intrigued with the Hawaiians' surfboards and their watermanship and at nine years old [1922] became one of the first dozen surfers on the Pacific Coast."

The surf culture in California was amoebic at this time. There were maybe 125 practicing surfers in California all through the 1920s, and because surfboards were so big and heavy and hard to transport, most surfers stored them at bathhouses. As a teenager, Peterson was influenced and mentored by two of the greats—Duke and

Blake, who were around the Santa Monica beach surfing and lifeguarding when they weren't competing in the Olympics or surfing in Hawai'i. You can only imagine the effect these two healthy, sturdy watermen had on a young man with Viking blood in his veins.

By 1932, Pete Peterson was nineteen years old, lean and fit and a good enough waterman to win the first of four victories in the Pacific Coast Surf Riding Championships. That same year, he and his pal, Whitey Harrison, set off for Hawai'i.

Peterson loved Hawai'i and the Hawaiians liked Peterson. "See, Pete spoke little and listened much," Whitey Harrison recalled to Craig Lockwood. "He could surf, all right. They liked that. And they liked the fact that he wasn't just another rich *haole*

Waikiki Brochure, 1930s
Surfing Heritage Foundation

off the Matson liner. He could use tools and make boards. His opinions were valued."

Peterson and Harrison had a time in Hawai'i. At one point they tried to hitchhike to the North Shore and ended up walking the Oahu Railroad tracks through miles of pineapple fields. When they got to the ocean, they saw a nasty wave breaking on a coral reef. Sure they couldn't surf it, they feared even swimming it and risking losing their trunks. So they stripped to nothing and swam out for an inspection of a wave that would later be called Banzai Pipeline.

The Wave That Would Become Pipeline wasn't the only revelation Peterson had on his first trip to Hawai'i. "Back in the winter of 1932," wrote Nat Young in *History of Surfing*, "Pete and Whitey surfed all over the south shore of Oahu, on every coral reef from Diamond Head to the entrance of Honolulu Harbor. They rode waves all day long on both boards and outrigger canoes, enjoying the unfamiliarly warm Hawaiian water. While surfing at Waikiki one morning, Pete spied an interesting looking board under another surfer. The statistics were about the same as his: 10' long by 2' wide, with a wide, square tail, but the timber was completely different. It was balsa. Back on the beach, Pete picked up one of these new, blond-colored boards and discovered they were half the weight of his redwood one. Apparently they had been made in Florida, and the balsa came from South America. They had been given several coats of varnish to keep the water out, but this tended to crack under pressure, especially where they were knelt upon. The weight was the quality that made these boards fantastic: only 30 to 40 pounds. Who made them is a mystery, as

Pacific System Homes Waikiki, 5'1"

With the rise of the Nazi Party in Germany and the start of World War II, Pacific System Homes renamed its Swastika model as the Waikiki in the late 1930s. This Waikiki is made of redwood and balsa. Adopted 2001.

are the surfers who rode them. But they represented such an advance on the old, heavy redwood boards that surfers began shaping their boards from the new timber, which soon began to be in great demand and hard to get."

Craig Lockwood backs this up in his article on Pete Peterson in *The Surfer's Journal*: "On returning from Hawai'i in 1933, Pete brings back an idea he'd seen and later reported to Peter Dixon, a former Santa Monica lifeguard, screenwriter, and surfing author. 'There's one error I'd like to bring out,' he tells Dixon. 'Some of the fellows who are supposed to be old-timers talk and write about the heavy redwood boards they were riding back in the 30s. They make it seem like we all lugged around those hundred-pounders. Well, gosh, that just wasn't so. A couple of guys from Florida, in the early 30s, built the first balsas and shipped them to Hawaii . . . and they were really keen. And when I came back after trying them, I started building balsa boards—ten-foot balsa boards that weighed under 20 pounds. They were that light because we didn't have fiberglass to cover them with. Later on, we added redwood noses and tail blocks (and rails) for strength, and that brought the weight up."

Pacific System Homes Waikiki, 5'11"

This thin bellyboard features a nose rocker for better dropping in. Made of balsa and redwood rails, this is a fine example of the later, 1940s Waikiki model. Adopted 1999.

Redwood and Pine Surfboard, 9'8"

A rare and fine example of the pre-balsa boards built in the late 1930s and early 1940s. It features several bolts along the width of the board to protect the board from coming apart. These bolts were then covered with wooden plugs. The board is original and unrestored. Adopted 2006.

CHAPTER 3

Sliding Ass

The Skeg and
the Hot Curl

1934 THROUGH
WORLD WAR II

I t was known derisively among surfers as "sliding ass."
Surfboards through the first thirty-five years of the twentieth century were so big and heavy they didn't really need
any more control. Riding those boards straight in on a wave at
Waikiki, there was no problem; the board rode true and you
could glide it all the way home. But try to cut a fast angle across
a wave, and there was no control. The tail of the surfboard slid,
and the surfer most often took the plunge. Sliding ass.

What was needed was a way to control the boards if surfing
was going to advance beyond simply riding waves "straight off,
Adolph." Something like a skeg, something like a Hot Curl.

Riding the Rudder

Again, it was Tom Blake who came up with the idea first. As
Blake's hollow boards became lighter and faster and more
refined, surf riding did the same. The surfers of Waikiki began
moving farther outside and riding the bigger days, and there
came a time when those squaretails needed some guidance.

"When I first went to the Islands, they used wide-tailed boards

Woody Brown, 1940s
*Woody Brown slides
right without sliding ass
on Oahu.* Mary Sue
Gannon and David L.
Brown Productions

Opposite Page:
Hot Curl Plank, 10'3"
*Made of redwood, balsa,
and pine in the 1930s, this
was likely an original Pacific
System Homes board
modified by tapering the
tail into a Hot Curl in order
to perform better in
Hawaiian waves. The board
was owned and surfed by
John Blyth around Oahu,
primarily on the breaks at
Waikiki and Makaha. It was
later purchased from John's
daughter, a resident of the
Big Island. Adopted 2004.*

Hot Curl, 10'8"

This late 1930s redwood Hot Curl board was shaped with a gun-like outline, which was very futuristic at that time. Boards of that era were usually just varnished, but due to the deteriorated nature of the wood here, it was later coated in resin and fiberglass for protection. Adopted 1995.

and they used to spinout on a steep, critical slide," Blake was quoted in the *Cowabunga!* exhibit at the Santa Monica Heritage Museum in 1994. "I figured it would be easy to correct that problem. Just add something—a keel. Finally, I got around to it. You didn't hurry things up over there. You were having too much fun surfing every day. Finally, I put a fin on the board and it worked fine. It was a shallow fin, about 4" deep and a foot long."

Blake further described this rudder for reporter Margaret Bairos, who wrote a

1936 article in the *Honolulu Advertiser* telling the world what Blake was up to: "My new hollow board is especially adapted for big waves, 25 to 30 feet high, what we call storm surf," Blake said. "It weighs 116 pounds; and in huge 30-foot waves, the metal handle at the stern end of the board allows a surfer to hold it in a break. The most recent development is the attaching of a stabilizer or fin at the bottom of the board at the stern. I got the idea from airships. It helps to steer or control the board."

Blake's first rudder—or "skeg," as it would be known—came off a wrecked motorboat. It was aluminum and 4 inches deep and 6 inches long. Too pitted and sharp to leave unexposed, Blake put a piece of *koa* wood over the fin and attached it to a 14-foot paddleboard. The first time he paddled it, all that directional stability felt weird and Blake thought it was all a bogus idea until he caught a wave: "I remember . . . having the thought, well, this board is—this thing's no good," Blake said to Gary Lynch in April 1989. "And I probably would have discarded it. I took it out and caught a pretty good wave on it, a six-foot wave, maybe, and it was remarkable the control you had over the board with this little skeg on it. It didn't spin out, it steered easy, because the tail held steady when you put the pressure on the front, and it turned any way you wanted it, and I knew right from that moment it was a success. But that was the only one in existence, and nobody else paid any attention to it, and it took ten years before that thing really caught on."

With the benefit of retrospect it's funny to see how long it took surfers to accept what is now so obvious.

Pacific System Homes, 10'0"

This late 1930s balsa-and-redwood board from Pacific System Homes was later modified with the addition of a skeg. The times they were a-changin'. Adopted 1996.

Hot Curl, 10'8"

A classic example of the redwood Hot Curl era of the late 1930s, with clean template lines and well transitioned foils. The tail is pulled in for the hollow surf in Hawai'i. Holes were drilled to attach a rope for ease in holding onto the board. This Hot Curl was originally owned by a Hawaiian family in the Kalihi Valley. It was ridden in Waikiki until the mid 1950s, and most likely surfed by Duke Kahanamoku at that time. Afterward, it was discarded in the family's backyard. Adopted 2003.

Origins of the Hot Curl

While Blake was first tinkering with his skeg in the mid-1930s, other Hawaiian surfers were dreaming up their own solutions to the heartbreak of "sliding ass." For surfer John Kelly, the answer was to use an axe.

"In 1934, Fran Heath and I were surfing at Brown's surf on a glassy day," Kelly told *The Surfer's Journal*'s Craig Stecyk.

"We couldn't turn our redwood planks fast enough to get out of the peak onto the shoulder and be able to catch the tube. The waves were about fifteen feet and they'd just pound us. On every wave we'd catch, if you tried to turn your board a little bit, the back end would come out because there was no skeg, and you'd just 'slide ass' sideways to the inside where you'd try to save it from the rocks and then paddle back out again. So we came back to my house on Black Point, and I had two saw horses set up on the porch. I took an axe and said, 'Damn it, how ever deep this axe goes I'm gonna cut that much off the side of the board.' So I let it fly and it went into the redwood, and we cut the rails down and made a board with a tail about five inches wide. Where the two sides came together at the bottom it became a sort of vee shape. Then we used the drawknife and a plane to smooth it down and sand it, and by mid-afternoon we were back out there with this board. I caught a wave and the tail just dug in and I went right across, and we figured something had happened."

What happened was directional stability and speed and a whole new world of waves and surfing that opened up by shrinking the width of the tail and creating a vee

Sliding Ass, 1930s
A surfer slides through a wave on his suddenly old-school Pacific System Homes board. Oh, for a skeg and a Hot Curl tail!
Photograph by Don James

that bit into the wave. That narrowed-down tail was the Hot Curl.

"The cutting down of the tail allowed us to immediately turn and trim high across the wave," surfer George Downing told Stecyk, "versus on the wide tailed boards having to first drop all the way to the bottom then pull all the way back up before angling. Plus when you tried to put a wide tailed plank into an angle high on the face and really pull in tight the tail would slide out. 'Slidin' ass' we called it. That's what caused John Kelly and Fran Heath to cut that first board down after 'slidin' ass' at Brown's in 1934.'"

Wally Froiseth continued the story to Craig Stecyk: "After that first board was cut down, John and I got so jazzed because we were going behind guys—it worked so good now. When you'd go in back of guys like Duke and Tom Blake everybody became interested and the thing really caught on."

Everybody tried their own solutions to sliding ass, chopping down big Pacific System Swastikas, shaping new pintailed boards. Froiseth remembered the array of oddball and customized boards that began to flourish. During the 1930s, he was one of a surf drunk crew of kids from Kahala who used Waikiki as their playground. Froiseth, Fran Heath, John Kelly, and their friends called their crew the "Empty Lot" gang: "At that time, every surfer knew every other surfer," Froiseth was quoted on www.legendarysurfers.com. "And, not only every other surfer, they knew every other surfboard. They knew exactly who owned the board. There were boards with initials and names and all kinds of crazy stuff and everybody had their own design."

Froiseth's favorite ride was his pintail redwood surfboard he had developed. With the big balsa-redwoods, he tried cutting down the tail and shaping a vee into it, but that didn't do the trick with those old-style boards. "It just didn't work that good because it was too buoyant," he remembered on www.legendarysurfers.com. "Even though the tail was narrow, it was thick and wouldn't sink in. It floated too high. I owned about the sixth or seventh balsa board in here [to the Hawaiian Islands]; I got it for tandems. We'd walk up the beach, ask some girl: 'Hey how about going surfing tandem?' In those days everybody would go out. . . . We never asked for any favours . . . we just wanted

Sliding Right, 1930s

A quartet of surfers slide ass smoothly to the right. Photograph by Don James

people to enjoy the sport. So I had my solid redwood and I had this balsa for tandem, you know."

Woody Brown arrived in Hawai'i around the time the Hot Curl was getting hot. "There were no skegs then," Woody recalled on www.legendarysurfers.com. "What's his name [Blake] had [invented it], but nobody used it. He put it on his hollow boards, because the hollow boards would slide tail, too. But Wally and those guys had no respect for the hollow board because it couldn't ride big waves. I mean, it was dynamite in a big wave. You know, the wave would just take it away like it was nothing; no control at all; too big and clumsy and flat. It would slide all around.

Of course, with a skeg, you could control it.

"Wally and them had small, little boards, about 9 to 10 feet, whereas the hollow boards were 12, 14, 15 feet. Duke's board was 20 feet long! It weighed 200 pounds! I couldn't even pick it up and carry it! Of course, it was wonderful for Castle. I mean, once that bugger dropped in, you know, and started going, you just hold on and try to stay with it. It would just take off!

"The hollow boards, they never used 'em in surf over 8 feet. After that, they were uncontrollable. So, Wally and them had great disdain for them. They wouldn't have anything to do with 'em. So, they wouldn't have anything to do with the keel either. 'What do you want a keel for?

Woody Brown, 1940s
Woody slides ass in Hawai'i, where he was one of the unsung innovators of surfboard design.

We don't need a keel.'

"Which was true! The Hot Curls didn't need a keel."

No one wanted to make that swim and everyone wanted to make waves. Pretty soon, way back in 1937, the Coconut Wireless began to vibrate with this new innovation, a board that would slide hot through the curl and not slide ass. "A lot of guys—like Whitey Harrison—when they came down and saw what our boards could do at Castle, him and Pete Peterson cut their tails down—right there on goddamn Waikiki Beach!" Woody was quoted on www.legendarysurfers.com "They cut their tails down. Of course, when they went back to the Coast, they took their boards with 'em."

Making New Waves

With their new Hot Curl boards, the Waikiki surfers began to look twice at waves they couldn't even have considered before. In the late 1930s, Froiseth and his Empty Lot crew took their boards over to the North Shore of Oahu to see if they could ride the winter waves that broke big and lonely on that side of the island: "Whitey Harrison, he and Tarzan Smith went out to Haleiwa one day," Froiseth was quoted in *The Surfer's Journal*. "This was, like, around '37 or '38, whatever it was. They went out to Haleiwa. It was a big day. And they both almost drowned. So, Gene Smith was telling us about this. 'Oh, Christ! You ought to see these waves!'

"Me and my gang, we hear that: 'Hey, let's go!' So, the next weekend we go out there, you know, but Haleiwa wasn't that good, but Sunset Beach was good, so we just went to Sunset. At that time, there wasn't a name or anything. We just saw a good surf and went out. It was just when we started to have our Hot Curl boards. My brother and I, Dougie Forbes, Fran, of course, Kelly; there were really only a couple of guys who went North Shore after Whitey and Gene.

"It was just too much for the other guys."

CHAPTER 4

Plastic Fantastic

Wondrous Shapes and Wonder Materials

POST–WORLD WAR II EXPERIMENTS

Doc Ball Hop Swarts Jim Reynolds
By Santa Cruz Surf Club 1943

Just as all Americans remember where they were when they heard Pearl Harbor was attacked, so can they remember where they were when they learned America had ended World War II by dropping some new kind of big bomb on Japan. In December 1945, Bob Simmons was out surfing a big south-swell day at Malibu when word came that the war was over. According to Pat O'Connor, an L.A. County lifeguard who was also around the beach, "Simmons ranted and raved all day that they would ruin the world with this new bomb. No one knew what it was, but Simmons knew something about its potential destructive powers."

If there was anyone in the surfing world who could fully grasp the implications of The Bomb, it was Simmons. At the time, he was working as a machinist for Douglas Aircraft, volunteering for the night shift so he could surf all day. Maybe Simmons was upset because he had it good, getting paid good wartime money with plenty of spare time to ride waves. Maybe he was worried about the crowds at Malibu if everyone came back all at once. Or maybe he understood what The Bomb was

Beach Boys, 1944
Hanging out at the Santa Cruz Surf Club during the World War II years were Doc Ball, Hop Swarts, and Jim Reynolds. Their monstrous old boards were about to become very old fashioned.
Doc Ball

Opposite Page:
Bob Simmons, 9'6"
The thoroughly modern surfboard, circa 1950. Made of solid balsa, it sported a single fin. This Bob Simmons board survived in its original condition, and is now very rare. Adopted 2002.

and had a Nostradamian glimpse of the future—the Cold War and the population boom in Southern California.

Either way, Simmons remains one of the most intelligent, innovative, foresighted, and eccentric men to ever set foot on a surfboard, and if you know the surfing world, that's saying a lot. Simmons began surfing in 1939 and died while surfing in 1954. But in that short fifteen years, he applied his exact, mathematical brain to the problems of making surfboards lighter, faster, stronger, and more maneuverable.

In short, Bob Simmons dropped a bomb of his own on the world of surfboard design.

Enter the Mad Scientist

Robert Wilson Simmons was born in 1919 in Los Angeles when the City of Angels was still the last best place. When he was seventeen, he was seriously hurt when a car crashed into his bicycle at the corner of Los Angeles' Beverly and Vermont streets. His doctor put a stainless wire loop in Simmons' elbow to lock the arm in a natural extended position, and told him to exercise the arm regularly or he'd lose it to amputation. After the doctor left, another patient—who in retrospect could be forgiven his nosiness—hobbled up on crutches with a casted broken leg: "You ought to try surfing," this unidentified surfer told Simmons, "because you paddle and swim a lot."

While recovering from the bicycle accident, Simmons applied to Caltech and passed the admittance exams, despite having no high school diploma. "Not for credit, but for knowledge," he used to tell friends. Simmons was entranced by aero- and hydrodynamics—by the way air and water flowed over, under, and around different

planes—and he wanted to be properly trained in the math of these phenomena.

It was 1939 when Simmons first got on a surfboard. While visiting his sister and her husband on Balboa Island, Simmons was towed by a speedboat into the waves along Newport Beach, riding an old Tom Blake paddleboard. Getting towed on a board with a trick arm is one thing, learning how to paddle and stand with a bad arm is another—especially when boards of the day weighed anywhere from 60 to 120 pounds. "I had to have a friend or my mother help me load the board on a car because it was so heavy," Simmons told his friend John Elwell. "I had to drag it down the beach. You couldn't turn them and they would pearl." Always an innovator, Simmons used a red wagon towed behind a bicycle to get his board to the beach, and before he had a car he hopped freight trains with his board to travel to surf spots along the coast.

During the war, Simmons got a job with Gard Chapin building garage doors, but also getting his first practical experience making surfboards. Chapin is best known in the surfing world as being the stepfather of 1960s surfing rebel Miki Dora, but he was also a tireless surfboard inventor in his own right. Chapin experimented with his own boards, trying out ideas, shaping them into wood, and then surfing them there and then. According to Malcolm Gault-Williams: "Gard Chapin significantly changed the accepted San Onofre style of rail. The plan shapes were similar to the old San Onofre outlines. Even as far back as pre–World War II, Gard was turning the rail down in the back and using nose blocks to give lift in the nose."

In those days, most surfboards were still made of redwood, balsa, mahogany, and other hardwoods—although there was

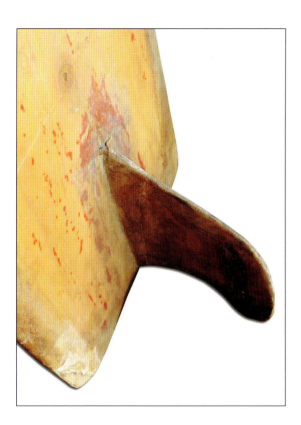

Bob Simmons, 9'6"

The thoroughly modern surfboard, circa 1950. Made of solid balsa, it sported a single fin. This Bob Simmons board survived in its original condition, and is now very rare. Adopted 2002.

also the hollow school, known as kookboxes because of the kooky way they handled. Simmons now began hollowing out planks as Tom Blake had done and began to riff on the foundation laid down by Chapin. Because most men were at war, the boards Simmons made were for kids, and so he concentrated on making them lighter and easier to handle. "To make money," Joe Quigg was quoted on www.legendarysurfers.com, "he had started remodeling old-fashioned boards for people."

Since Chapin built garage doors from plywood, Simmons had access to the bonded wood as well as a lot of other different, modern materials. "Simmons finally came up with this—probably the first production line other than Pacific Systems—the first production line surfboard that had a foam [expanded poly-

Bob Simmons, 10'0"
A classic example of the radical surfboard design innovations introduced by Simmons. This board was shaped in 1949–1950 from solid balsa. It was originally owned by the uncle of Wally Milican, who bought it from Simmons. In 1989, Wally traded it to Greg Noll for some of his boards. Adopted 2001.

styrene] core, balsawood rails, and plywood deck," said innovative 1950s and 1960s surfboard shaper Reynolds Yater, quoted on www.legendarysurfers.com. "He came up with that idea probably because of all the influence he had from plywood . . . mahogany veneers on the outside to get them even lighter. He did incredible things for the time he did them in, compared to today." Because of Simmons' draft status and flexible employment, he was about the only guy anybody could buy boards from during those war years.

As Rennie Yater continued, "If anybody was ever to get the credit of being the 'Father of the Modern Surfboard,' I would say it would have to be Simmons. He changed board design in a shorter period of

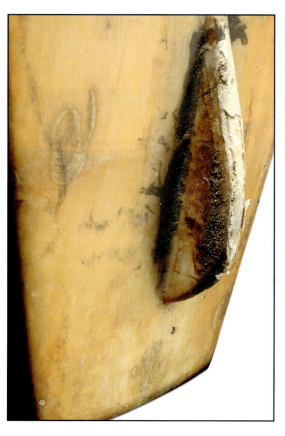

Balsa Board, 9'10"

The original shaper of this board is unknown, but he or she was obviously influenced by the contemporary designs of Bob Simmons, Joe Quigg, and Matt Kivlin. The board was likely made circa 1948–1950. It's covered in original "airplane" cloth fiberglass. Unrestored. Adopted 2005.

time than anybody has before or since. When his boards started showing up at San Onofre, they couldn't believe it. Such a traditional place. Everything had to look the same, ride the same, pose the same. . . . Simmons' boards weren't welcome at San Onofre. See, his influence was more at Malibu. He could care less about the San Onofre area. He always went up and tested his stuff at Malibu or Palos Verdes Cove."

Simmons began showing up at Malibu with his boards, swimming them out because it was more efficient than paddling. Simmons was a decade older than most of the young crew at Malibu, who would grow up to become influential surfers and shapers—Peter and Corny Cole, Buzzy Trent, Joe Quigg, and Matt Kivlin.

Bob Simmons never attempted to fully explain his designs to anyone because they were "complex and the applications were simple, and could be modified," remembered John Elwell in *The Surfer's Journal*. "He was also secretive and didn't trust some people." Simmons' brother, Dewey, had had a long legal battle over his invention of an electrical strain gauge, and this was probably ever-present in Simmons' mind. Elwell also recalled, "There was also some delight in baffling some of the rule of thumb, surfing know-it-alls. There was no doubt he rejected exaggerators and dreamers on the beach. He gravitated to the better surfers and ignored the less serious and unskilled."

The Wild Ones

On July 4, 1947, the sleepy town of Hollister, California, was invaded by bikers from the Booze Fighters Motorcycle Club. They celebrated the holiday in an infamous drunken orgy that inspired the Marlon Brando film *The Wild Ones*. Dale

Velzy was a member of the Booze Fighters MC, and would have been at Hollister too if not for a mechanical failure. Looking back, Dale Velzy *was* Marlon Brando—handsome, tough, smart, a dude dresser, good with women. Velzy was a rebel, but his cause was to revolutionize the production, performance, and marketing of surfboards from the 1940s into the 1950s.

Dale Velzy was born in September 1927 in Hermosa Beach, and hailed from a Dutch family that had always been involved in logging, woodworking, and cabinetmaking. During the Depression years of his childhood, while his family struggled, Velzy found free fun at the ocean, starting surfing "when I was just a little squirt," as he told Malcolm Gault-Williams.

His woodworker father made Velzy his first board when Velzy was eight or nine. "It was really heavy and I had to drag it down to the surf," Velzy related to his biographer, Paul Holmes, in the book *Dale Velzy is Hawk*. "Every couple of months he'd reshape it into something better. Finally he got one there that really worked for me and I really got into surfing. . . . When we'd travel to the different beaches, I'd find a new design one of the older guys was using; we'd go home and try to shape something like it. I got into building boards like that, shaping down old planks into smaller, lighter boards I could use. . . . There were a bunch of us little kids [getting into surfing]. But I had the advantage of cutting my boards down. They were just riding hand-me-downs. They weren't thinning them down and giving them tail rocker[s]. And my boards were lighter. Every time you cut two feet off the tail of one of those planks you were losing 40 pounds!"

Velzy also experimented with fins in the late 1930s, using dowels and wood

Gary Linden Agave Board, 9'6"
Hand-shaped by Gary Linden, this board was inspired by a Bob Simmons board owned by Bird Huffman, a Windansea local. Gary also made the blank, with hand-harvested agave wood from the La Jolla area. Adopted 1998.

screws to fasten on rudders that were 12 inches long and 3 inches high. These were low-tech skegs, but better than sliding ass.

Surfing turned Velzy into a full-time truant by the time he was fifteen, inspiring his parents to send their rebel lad to the Southern California Military Academy with its stiff boots, stiff uniforms, and even stiffer system of demerits. Velzy lasted about a week, ran away, got caught, got punished. When he was sixteen, he was too young to be drafted but eligible to join the Merchant Marine with parental permission. In September 1943, he enlisted, saw the world, and came back with ideas that would change the surfboard forever.

Velzy qualified as an ordinary seaman, shipped out, and got a good look at the Hawaiian surfing technology of the time, and found there wasn't much difference between Waikiki and the mainland.

The boards that turned Velzy's head were the Hot Curls, and when he returned to California he translated all he had seen through his hands into redwood and balsa. Velzy bought the raw materials at General Veneer in South Gate, California, and glued up blanks of balsa for lightness, adding harder redwood for the rails and tail block. Velzy used the traditional woodworking tools of his father: saw, adze, drawknife, and jackplane to take down and finish the board, finishing them with varnish. Anyone who has varnished a wooden boat knows that it's a lot of work, and back in 1945, the varnish had to be heated in a pot, brushed on, allowed to dry, sanded lightly, and then repeated many times over. All in all, it required two full weeks of work to build those boards given the materials and equipment of the day.

This experience building two boards soon turned into a business. Word spread, and Velzy began repairing and reshaping planks for others. Most of the boards surfers brought him were Pacific System Homes Swastikas, called Waikiki models post-Hitler. The boards were well crafted and stylish, but too heavy and not suited for beach breaks or high-performance riding.

Velzy's business grew, and it also gave him a chance to experiment, changing the rounded noses to pointed noses and doing the same thing on the other end.

With his rebel past, Velzy was also part of a new rebellious wave in surfing. In the postwar years, a lot of guys were enjoying the G.I. Bill and the 52/50—the veterans' stipend that handed them $50 a week for 52 weeks, about the same as a modern unemployment check. This gave them the cash to hang out, surf, get into trouble. At Hermosa Beach, this led to a crackdown as the cops insisted Velzy stop littering the beach and pier with his balsa shavings. Up the coast a ways, the Manhattan Beach police simply threw most of the surfers in jail, insisting they clean up their act. That sweep resulted in the formation of the Manhattan Beach Surfing Club.

Velzy joined the MBSC where he influenced a lot of young minds, including Bing Copeland and Greg Noll, who were groms when Velzy was the coolest thing on the beach—red-hot women, ice-cold beer. "Everything went to hell with the introduction of the lightweight surfboard," Greg Noll said in Stacy Peralta's *Riding Giants*. "The generation before, those guys were all gentlemanly, but with the introduction of balsa wood and fiberglass and resin and lightweight boards, it was like someone threw a light switch, and everything changed."

Scarfs, Rockers, and Miracle Materials

While surfing one day at Palos Verdes, Dale Velzy met Bob Simmons—or more correctly, Velzy spotted Simmons' surfboard. This board sported a spoon-shaped plywood extension on the nose designed to give the board extra lift—a "scarfed" nose. And, equally important, this extension was fastened to the nose with what was then a high-tech composite material, fiberglass.

Fiberglass and polyester resin were two miracles of technology that came out of World War II. Surfboard shaper Stephen Shaw, who wrote the first published manual on surfboard making, 1963's *The Surfboard Builder's Manual*, explained: "Fiberglass is a glass similar to window glass heated to a molten state and strained through very small platinum discs into the air and collected as very fine threads." When the fiberglass was covered in molten resin and left to dry, the combination created a light yet strong material that would change surfboards forever. Fiberglas, as the trade name had it, was invented for home insulation in 1938 by Russell Games Slayter of Owens-Corning. Polyester resin was developed by DuPont in 1936, but the process was refined by German scientists during World War II. British spies stole the secrets and handed them off to the U.S. government, and by 1942, American Cynamid was producing polyester resin for use with fiberglass cloth. Bob Simmons knew about fiberglass from his wartime work at Douglas Aircraft, and in 1946, he began exposing the secret to fellow shapers like Velzy.

Building a surfboard from this new wonder material was not easy. Simmons and others experimented endlessly, often with frustrating results. "The first resin manufacturer was the Bakelite Corporation," Nat Young wrote in *The History of Surfing*. "Those early resins were the same viscosity as the resins used today but the catalyst was a paste-like Vaseline that had to be thoroughly mixed with the resin. The drying time was totally dependent on the amount of sunshine and naturally one side dried while the rails were still tacky. Because it made the boards look ugly compared to the shiny varnish already available it took a little time to gain acceptance, but because resin was much more protective, change was inevitable." Trying to solve these mysteries, surfboard shaper Joe Quigg asked such detailed questions at Los Angeles chemical companies that he was suspected of being a German spy.

Pete Peterson may have been the first to build a full board from fiberglass, according to Young. With aid from Brant Goldsworthy, Peterson's fiberglass surfboard was ready to ride in June 1946. "The board was constructed of two hollow moulded halves joined together with a redwood central stringer and with the seam sealed with fiberglass tape," Young wrote.

Simmons, meanwhile, was using the fiberglass to supplement his investigations into surfboard shapes. Sometime in 1946, Santa Monica surfers Quigg and Dave Rochlen visited Simmons in Pasadena, where he was doing his R&D in a garage. "When we first met Simmons, we knew he was different," Rochlen recalled. "We knew he was somehow special, and we knew he was up to something. We called him a mad scientist." John Elwell, writing in *The Surfer's Journal*, elucidated: "Some radical changes in Simmons' boards occurred after 1946. The rails were coming down, and tails and noses were thinner. They were still modified planks. . . . He designed with his machinist's skills a surfboard-shaping machine that would rough shape his blanks. . . . Simmons was still building big, heavy redwood planks but he was beginning to futz around with plastics."

Simmons continued working on the "scarfed" nose, putting fiberglass over an extra piece of wood to give the nose lift and prevent pearling. Velzy and others began working with balsa to put "rocker" into the noses of surfboards. A flat surfboard has no rocker at all and almost all planks were dead flat. Rocker is the curve going out from the midpoint of the board to the nose and the tail to provide maneuverability in the back end and prevent pearling in the front.

Simmons was also refining his planks as perhaps only a surf-stoked Caltech dropout would. He thinned them down, applying sophisticated planing hull theories, doing all he could to make the boards lighter, faster, and more maneuverable. An invaluable sixteen minutes of 16-milimeter film—since christened *Sweet Sixteen*—shot by Malibu resident John Larronde in 1947 shows surfing as it was at Malibu, San Onofre, Rincon, and Ventura Overhead. Watching that footage, there are a lot of guys going very fast and straight on those boards, but there are only a few rudimentary turns—cutbacks like a 747 changing direction. When you take off on a perfect six-foot wave at Rincon or Malibu you want to make that wave as best you can.

And when surfing a big day at Overhead, you want a board you can rely on to make sections and go fast and not slide out, because a lost board then meant a long, cold, lonely swim to the beach. It was most likely a combination of perfect California surf combined with Simmons' slight gimpy-arm handicap from his childhood bicycle crash that inspired his effort to make boards faster, lighter, better.

To these ends, Simmons was also experimenting with Styrofoam. Polystyrene foam was used during World War II, molded into airplane-fuselage radar domes. Simmons tracked down the raw chemical from a government or corporate agency. He fashioned a cement mold in the ground and blew his own foam. The mold was topped with a plywood lid, five large rocks holding it in place. As reported by John Elwell in *The Surfer's Journal*, "We saw the blanks in 1950 at the lifeguard station at Imperial Beach. The mold still exists by a barn on his late uncle's and aunt's ranch in Norwalk. He did a lot of private research and development there, kept tools, storage and a large work space."

Simmons also had a new discovery, an item that wasn't secret, but it was likely over the heads of most shapers. A naval architect with a doctorate from MIT named Lindsey Lord published an intensive study on planing hulls. His research defined these as hulls designed to climb toward the water surface as power is applied, reducing the friction or drag of the water and therefore increasing speed. It's obvious why such research was essential to the Navy, but likely only Simmons had the brain and background to understand how such physics applied to surfboards. "Lord's study was remarkable," John Elwell was quoted on www.legendarysurfers.com. "The navy had sought an ideal width and length shape for quick lift, maneuverability and speed. Lord maintained the study was solid information and a new, not previously known, naval science. Simmons must have been delighted. The book was full of graphs, complex equations and recommended a new material to strengthen lightweight planing hulls: fiberglass and resin. The form developed was simple parallelism, with an ideal length-width ratio number called aspect ratio, used in wing design. . . .One of the problems, Lord relates, concerned the ideal shape. It was not attractive, but could be. He mentions that pointed sterns produce the most drag, extreme lightness is dangerous, and planing hulls are complex. He

416 - 31st STREET, NEWPORT BEACH

Joe Quigg and Dale Velzy Decals

warned that a few weird things work, but don't be fooled. . . . Everything modified to get something else . . . is a compromise. All things were considered and applied for the ultimate goal of superlative speed; such as the nature of water, skimming on it, Newton's Laws, Bernoulli's Law of Lift, resistance, load, attack angles, rudder designs and center of gravity. The book was the mother lode for Simmons. Many surfers saw it in Simmons' possession, but couldn't understand it, much less apply it to surfboards." Inspired, Simmons also spent hours at the Scripps Institute of Oceanography, gleaning information on wave forecasting developed by the navy, who needed such tools to help strategize beach landings and other operations. He had other uses for this information.

Applying these wartime technologies to surfboards caused a few wars of their own around California. Combining the planing-hull technology with fiberglass, Simmons and Gard Chapin began making surfboards that blazed past everyone else. Simmons claimed the scarfed nose gave the board extra lift to prevent pearling by making it plane. Those who saw the wisdom in Simmons' modifications hired him to work magic on their own planks, scarfing a piece on the nose and fairing it in to create nose lift.

Simmons and Chapin rode their boards up and down the coast, from Malibu to San Onofre and beyond, places like Tijuana Sloughs and Santa Cruz. They were "proclaiming planing hull design," Elwell recalled. "Those who got in the way and did not heed their abusive warnings were rammed." Yet other surfers—especially those who had just returned from the fire pits of Germany and the Pacific—weren't going to take lip

from a haughty, rear-echelon gimp with a bad arm: "Simmons was dunked and beaten up in Malibu, punched down at San Onofre and stoned on the trail to Palos Verdes Cove," Elwell said. "He returned in the evening with an axe and drove it into some paddleboards that were lying around; ostensibly belonging to the stoners." Palos Verdes has since become legendary for acts of localism—stoning visiting surfers, vandalizing their cars—and Simmons might have been one of the first victims when the Palos Verdes Cove crew vandalized boards on Simmons' jalopy in retaliation.

Working out of Norwalk, Simmons began surfing San Diego more often instead. Maybe he chose San Diego because it was less crowded. Maybe it was because he could test his materials and designs in relative privacy.

Marilyn and Darrilyn

In those golden years at Malibu, a new surfing crowd was forming that was equally golden. Tommy Zahn was perhaps the most gilded of the men, a first-rate waterman who was movie-star handsome, and had in fact been hired at 20th Century Fox. And around him was a love triangle with studio head Darryl Zanuck's daughter, Darrilyn, and another young surfer girl by the name of Norma Jean Baker.

Not surprisingly, Zahn never forgot the woman who would become Marilyn Monroe. He told of Norma Jean and those wondrous days in the book *Goddess: The Secret Lives of Marilyn Monroe* by Anthony Summers: "She was in prime condition, tremendously fit. I used to take her surfing up at Malibu—tandem surfing, you know, two riders on the same surfboard. I'd take her later, in the dead of winter when it

Marilyn, 1940s

While the surfers concentrate on their guitars and ukes, a cute young bobby soxer named Norma Jean (later Marilyn Monroe) sits all by her lonesome at a beach party. Knowing surfers, it was probably just a momentary aberration. Photographer Unknown.

was cold, and it didn't faze her in the least; she'd lay in the cold water, waiting for the waves. She was very good in the water, very robust, so healthy, a really fine attitude towards life. I was twenty-two when I met her, and I guess she was twenty. Gosh, I really liked her."

Alas, love triangles rarely have happy endings, and this one was no different. As the legend goes, a jealous Darrilyn Zanuck might have got both Zahn and Norma Jean fired from 20th Century Fox. In the end, Marilyn became a movie star and legend, and Darrilyn only became the Eve of the modern shortboard.

At some time while the love was still hot during summer 1947, Zahn asked Joe Quigg to make a "novice girls' board" for Darrilyn. It had to be short and light, easy for a young woman to carry, and it had to fit in the back of a Town and Country convertible. And so Darrilyn would become the original Gidget. As Quigg was quoted on www.legendarysurfers.com, "She was at Malibu, really the first girl to buy a surfboard and buy a convertible and stick the surfboard in the back and drive up to Malibu and drive up and down the coast and learn to surf. Of the Malibu girls she was the first Malibu girl to really do it."

Joe Quigg was born in 1922 in Los Angeles and was bodysurfing in the Santa Monica shorebreak by the time he was six, falling in love with the ocean at a young age. Like Velzy's father, Quigg's dad was also a woodworker during a time when Los Angeles was being built. There was lumber everywhere around Quigg from early on—they were burning it in pyres to get rid of it—and so he grabbed a piece and used one of his dad's saws to fashion his first paddleboard when he was just 12. Since then, Quigg became one of the leading innovators in shaping surfboards, bending the old flat outlines into modern boards with rocker.

Now, he was commissioned to build a special board for his best friend's girl. So Quigg picked the best redwood and balsa from five different lumberyards and made a 10-foot 2-inch redwood-balsa with 50/50 rails, curved rail rocker, a flat planing bottom, and a fin. The board was soon nominated "the loosest board on the West Coast," and you wonder how much Darrilyn actually got to ride it as every guy on the beach wanted to try out this hot new board. The board was even lighter than the most advanced Simmons model, maybe because Simmons still thought heavier was better. Quigg said the board had "the complete combination," and he called it The Easy Rider: "I'd been building girls' boards since early '47," Quigg told Paul Holmes for *Dale Velzy is Hawk*. "It helped the girls to leave the tails wide. I'd put what I called easy-rider rocker in them. They were real easy to ride. A lot of girls learned how to surf on those boards in just a few months." And according to legend, after Zahn and Darrilyn broke up, Darrilyn had to raid Zahn's garage to get the board back.

In August 1947, the Los Angeles surf crew took a surfari down to San Onofre, Dave Rochlen, Matt Kivlin, and Pete Peterson borrowing that "novice girls' board." The Darrilyn Easy Rider board was faster and more maneuverable than anything else in the water. "It is immediately apparent that Rochlen is turning four times faster and making it into and out of what would previously have been inconceivable situations," Craig Stecyk wrote. "Pete Peterson next borrows the board, and is instantly banking and turning in an obvious departure from his patented power trim, runaway style." With this board, the crew proceeded to invent California hotdogging, right then and there.

The Hawaiian Connection

How are you going to keep 'em down on the farm after they've surfed Waikiki?

Tommy Zahn was the first of that crew to make the postwar passage to Honolulu, followed soon after by his buddies Quigg, Rochlen, and Kivlin. They brought their new, hot-rodded California boards with them—only to learn a lesson on surfboard design in Hawai'i's big waves.

Woody Brown was on the beach in 1947 running a catamaran service when this new group of wayfaring surfers showed up: "Tommy Zahn used to surf with us," Woody Brown was quoted on www.legendary-surfers.com. "I remember him at Waikiki and he had a balsa board. It was a very light balsa board. See, my board was 80 pounds for those big waves. He had a little board. It couldn't have weighed more than about 30 pounds; all balsa, nothing else. But, it was no good at all at Waikiki, see, with that trade wind blowing."

Hawaiian surfer Rabbit Kekai befriended the Malibu set, and rode their bizarre boards with the flat bottoms, 50/50 rails, and turned-down hard rails in the tails. His term for the wide-tail boards summed up their usefulness in Hawaiian waters— "mushers." "We were amazed to see them on those boards," Kekai said of the quiver brought over by the new *haole* invasion. "They were just standing at the back end on them because they had those wide tails with just one skeg in the center or concave tails with twin fins. Rochlen and Quigg had twin fins. Kivlin had one of his own single finned boards with a narrower tail." In the end, Quigg overheard the same refrain time and again, the local surfers shaking their heads and saying, "Oh, all that balsa—what a waste."

Quigg had a look around the Hawai'i scene during that winter of 1947 and what he saw translated through his innovative designer brain into new surfboard shapes. "Rabbit and I traded boards one day at Queen's," Quigg recalled to Craig Stecyk for *The Surfer's Journal.* "Rabbit was really skinny when he was young and probably didn't weigh much at all, so I got on his board and it just sank. I could stand on it in chest-deep water and his Hot Curl would press to the bottom and lay right on the reef." But where Quigg sank, Kekai flew. "Rabbit really started this style that they call hotdogging," Quigg continued to Craig Stecyk. "In the summer, Queen's would get overhead and Rabbit would be inside of the tube hanging five with no fin and his back arched. All you would see was this flying green blur visible through the lip of the wave. He'd do it over and over again, always with precision. The Island kids were doing amazing things on all kinds of their finless boards, but no one ever gave them credit. Rabbit would come flying out of the section, stomp on the tail

real hard and stand the board straight up on its tail and bring it down on a different angle and then run to the nose and take off in another direction."

Quigg also got a taste of Makaha on that first trip over: "I can remember paddling out at Makaha in point conditions and pushing up through the lip on a big set wave," Quigg said "Right at the top, as I'm about to punch through, I looked down and there was Georgie [Downing] standing there smiling, going faster than hell on his redwood. He was just streaking along in impossible situa-

Going Hawaiian, 1940s
With the surf beckoning, Tommy Zahn and Joe Quigg pause for a moment to pose with a board, Diamond Head looming in the distance.

tions and making it because of positioning and all that inertia. Downing pioneered the riding of really big, nasty waves."

Surfing was changing fast, and surfboards were changing just as quickly. Rabbit Kekai recalled to Craig Stecyk in *The Surfer's Journal*: "We got our board length coming down, really trimmed with 4-inch tails and pointed nose, and brought in to like 18 or 19 inches. They were pointers like the modern day gun,

that's how we had our boards: redwood planks with a V tail. For the big ones at Makaha, where we used to go a lot, we'd go out with the width to 20 or 20 1/2 inches. At Makaha, you'd drop in, point and go . . . make it through the bowl and do cutbacks and S turns on the inside. At Queens when we used to, ya know, get the hotdog deal going, my board was like 7 or 7 1/2 feet, sometimes up to 9 feet. I used to write 'Chi-Chi Bobo' on them."

The Need for Speed

On the passage over to Hawai'i on the SS *Lurline*, Quigg had sketched a new board he made during the summer that he nicknamed Pintail #1. He was dreaming of the fastest board possible, and his drawing shows a finned and streamlined pintail gun. Putting the sketch into wood, he cut a board in half end to end, removed 2 inches to slice the width from 23 to 21 inches, and then glued it back together. It was a foiled-down wide pintail with perhaps the first fiberglass fin, a carved-in rail rocker, low sharp rails, flowing rocker end to end, and a breakaway tail. Pintail #1 was launched at Malibu on June 11, 1947, just before Quigg built the Darrylin Easy Rider Board. As Matt Warshaw described it in his *Encyclopedia of Surfing*, Quigg "created the first pintail board, designed to hold traction at higher speeds; Quigg's pintail was the forerunner of the big-wave board."

Back from Hawai'i, he began sketching a new pintail. "Joe decided to cut the center out of his pintail and reattach the rails," Craig Stecyk wrote in *The Surfer's Journal*. "Thus making a narrower board. Kivlin and Quigg returned to Malibu where they reported the virtues of finless hot curl sliding to a skeptical public. This pintail was a forward-thinking innovation which featured an absolutely flat bottom with low rails rolling down to a sharp edge in the rear. This revolutionary board was basically ignored by all those present. Furthermore, if it were not for Quigg's considerable surfing ability, an outside move like this design could have led to total ostracization from the point elite."

In May 1948, Quigg built Pintail #2. He categorized it as a "speed board" and the "first narrow pintail." The board boasted a primal spearlike profile, with a flat bottom, low sharp rails, and a 100 percent breakaway tail. It would later become recognized as the Adam of the modern, big-wave pintail gun, a board that was about to come in very handy at Makaha, and would be further improved by the coming innovations in polyurethane foam.

**Joe Quigg Balsa
"Darrylin Zanuck" Gun, 9'10"**

Legendary builder Joe Quigg hand-shaped this replica of the famous "Darrylin Zanuck" board in 2003 from a chambered balsa blank. This is the same design that Quigg shaped in 1947 for surfing big Rincon in California. The shape was way ahead of its time, featuring the same 50/50 rails, pintail, and progressive rocker used in today's boards. Quigg calls it the "complete combination," his single most important contribution to the surfing world. The original board— then tested by Dave Rochlen, Tommy Zahn, and Pete Peterson—was instantly judged as a breakthrough in shaping design. Along with Bob Simmons and Matt Kivlin, Quigg is justly considered the father of the modern surfboard. Adopted 2005. Photograph by Larry Hammerness

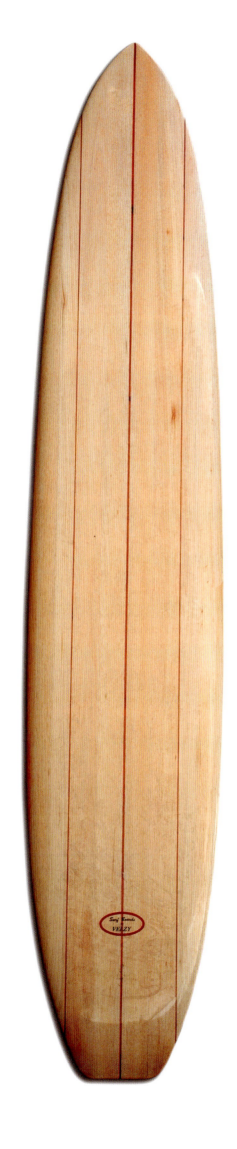

CHAPTER 5

Foam

Sandwich Boards,
Spoons, and
the Foam Future

FROM THE FALL
OF HITLER TO THE
RISE OF GIDGET

Blank Monday, December 5, 2005, a day that will live in infamy. Gordon "Grubby" Clark announced the immediate closure of his company, Clark Foam, and sent the surfboard industry sliding ass. Clark Foam had been *the* supplier of foam blanks going back to the late 1950s. Now, Clark broke up his concrete molds, leaving them like a graveyard of scattered tombstones—and marking what many saw as the death of the surfboard industry. Clark's abrupt, guarded decision was akin to Microsoft suddenly declaring it was offering no more software and the world's PCs suddenly going dark. Or OPEC ceasing oil production. Or the sun freezing over. Through a combination of ruthlessness and ruthless efficiency, Clark had shaken out all other contenders and claimed a near-monopoly on a market estimated to be anywhere from 400,000 to 600,000 blanks a year. At a minimum of $50 a blank, that's a $20 million to $30 million market. Now came Blank Monday as Clark pulled the plug.

Polyurethane foam began to bubble and pop as the ideal replacement for redwood and balsa in the period between the

Greg Noll Logo

Opposite Page:
Dale Velzy Pig, 9'0"
Modeled after one of the most famous surfboard shapes of all time, this is a modern rendition hand-shaped by Dale Velzy of his classic 1950s "Pig" shape. It's made from a balsa blank. Adopted 2002.

Joe Quigg Malibu Chip, 7'7"
Made of solid balsa, this is a boy's Malibu Chip from the 1950s. The board is unique and rare. Adopted 2003. Photograph by Larry Hammerness

fall of Hitler and the rise of Gidget. With the advent of foam, suddenly all other surfboard technology was history. The modern surfboard was the product of the Petrochemical Age and the miracles of fiberglass, polyester resin, and foam, all of which had their beginnings in wartime technological advances. Now, foam ruled.

Foam is based on an isocyanide mixed with a polyester or polyol, along with a complicated blend of catalyst and bubble-producing agents. Two chemical reactions take place simultaneously when the ingredients are mixed. One is the formation of the polyurethane. The other is a gas formed either through heat or through two chemicals forming carbon dioxide, yielding tiny bubbles within that polyurethane liquid. The bubbles expand and make the foam as the polyurethane is being formed within the mold. Once the mix is in the mold, it is baked for some thirty minutes, curing the foam. The molded blanks can now be sold to small-shop shapers or large-scale manufacturers for final shaping and glassing. As Grubby Clark noted in *Surfing Magazine*, "There's no romanticism in foam. We're just a raw materials supplier. It's dirty, messy and it's hard work and it's not anything you particularly dream of doing for a career. It's probably one of the worst operations involved in making a surfboard because it's fumy and smelly and you've got to work fast."

Foam boasted distinct advantages over redwood and balsa because it was readily available, lighter, and cheaper, and it could be molded into any shape or form. Surfboards would never be the same. Nor would the surfboard-shaping business.

Out of World War II and into the 1950s, there are numerous claims and cross-claims as to who used what first—and who stole what from whom when. As quickly as foam came in, the good old days of shapers sharing their secrets were gone. Foam changed surfboards, and helped percolate the new multi-million-dollar surf industrial complex along the way.

Early Styrofoam Experiments—and Failures

The earliest claim to experimenting with foam surfboards was made by Dave Sweet. In an interview with *The Surfer's Journal* publisher Steve Pezman, Sweet said he began playing with polystyrene foam in 1945—what was known as Styrofoam.

A Los Angeles native, Sweet grew up surfing from his family's beach cottage at Topanga Canyon. As he got older, Sweet moved up to Malibu. "Back then, if the surf was six feet, you'd get in your car and go to Malibu and there'd be maybe Buzzy, Rochlen and Timmy Lyons," Sweet said to Pezman. "And that was it! That was crowded."

Sweet learned to surf on the technology of the time: "At first I borrowed a Pacific Systems Homes," he said to Pezman. "Then I had one. Then shortly afterward, Bob Simmons built me a board. It weighed 120 pounds. It was constructed of redwood strips with inlaid balsa where you kneeled. The nose was Mexican primavera, a hardwood. That had to be 1946. After that I bought Bob's personal board. It was balsa and fiberglass, the very beginning. That was in about 1948. I was on the beach with my friend, Fred Harrison, and Simmons arrived with the first balsa fiberglass board, and Fred bought the board just like that. Then he came out with horrible boards. I think Matt Kivlin might have helped him. They were Styrofoam and plywood. To bond to Styrofoam they had to coat it with white glue, and I think it was a matter of delaminating, because people would go

JOIN THE BIG SWITCH - - -

Another of the Dave Sweet Surf Team --
ERIC THORNBURGH, MALIBU, Sept. '65

DAVE SWEET

CUSTOM BOARDS
SANTA MONICA CALIFORNIA

CONCAVES
And Nose Riding Concaves
At No Additional Cost.

DAVE SWEET SURFBOARDS
1402 OLYMPIC BLVD.
SANTA MONICA, CALIF.

FREE DELIVERY IN CONTINENTAL U.S.

EXCLUSIVE
VALLEY DEALER
FOR

SURF BOARDS
Dewey Weber

FOUR FAMOUS SHAPES

• Combination   • Speed
• Iggy Model And The All New
PERFORMER

Also
BELLY BOARDS
SURF ACCESSORIES

Surfboards

NEW—USED—REPAIRS

*All repairs are done in shop and
guaranteed*

Winter Hours: 12:30 to 6:00 p.m.
Saturday: 9:00 to 6:00

BEACH
Surf Shop

**4438 RESEDA BLVD.
TARZANA, CALIF.
(213) 343-9300**

Decals 20c and 35c

what it was. I surfed it one winter at Rincon, and, I think, for maybe a year and a half at Malibu. It worked fine."

Sweet claims this was all going on around 1945–1946 at the same time as Simmons, Joe Quigg, and others were looking into foam's possibilities. These early experiments were failures because of the nature of the materials. Styrofoam reacted badly with polyester resin, and so they had to use epoxy.

Quigg, meanwhile, was still trying to make Styrofoam fly. In 1947, he went against Simmons' thinking about heavy boards, and made a prototype, all-foam surfboard that was 4 feet long, with 4-ounce fiberglass. Over the next few years, he hacked a few feet off the best paddleboard designs and got deeper into the use of foam cores, coated with fiberglass and resin.

Simmons also began producing boards in 1947 and 1948 with a foam core of polystyrene, balsawood rails, and a plywood deck. By 1948, Simmons had a protoype board down to just 9 pounds that he was testing at the Caltech test tank. "Simmons was reported to be going so fast that his boards would become airborne and go out of control," noted Simmons' buddy, John Elwell. "He had pushed the high-aspect ratio and lightness to the limit. To correct this he increased weight and rebalanced his boards. The new boards had unusual features. They were vastly lighter. The noses and tails were thin and featured hydrofoiled rails. They were wide and with wide, slightly pulled-in tails. The nose had an increased turn-up with a camber and slight belly in them." Simmons called these "hydrodynamic planing hulls." And as was typical, he would not elaborate further, but it was obvious the boards combined elements never seen before.

out surfing, come in, stand their board up, and it would just sprong apart in the heat of the sun."

Styrofoam wasn't happening, and like Tom Blake and a lot of surfing innovators who had come before, Sweet went looking for a better way. In 1945 he built a board using extruded Styrofoam. Sweet ordered his raw materials from Dow Chemical in Michigan, but it was different from the foam Simmons used for his foam cores a few years later: "I just wanted to prove that a foam board . . . you could surf it," Sweet said to Pezman. "I had to use epoxy, and I glassed it and I colored it so nobody knew

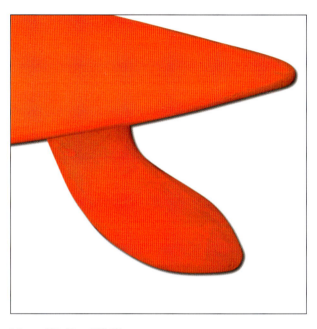

Matt Kivlin, 9'10"

In 1952, Kivlin shaped two near-identical boards. One is this red board; the other one is green, which Kivlin still owns. He also built a similar one but with a 10-inch tail for his then wife. They soon divorced, and the whereabouts of that board are unknown. As Kivlin stated, "Most of the boards that I shaped during the mid 1950s were for myself and a few friends. I was busy with my architectural career and had little time for a surfboard sideline . . . They had a new fin design that made them the only boards that didn't spin out at Rincon when the surf was hig" This board came from Jim Menge, the original buyer of the board in 1952. He had moved from Southern California years ago, and took the board along with him to Arkansas. Kivlin also shaped a copy of the narrow-tail version in 2004 and donated it to a Surfrider fundraiser. Adopted 2005.

Bob Simmons, 10'6"
Simmons custom-shaped this board from solid balsa in 1953 for Coronado lifeguard Wayne Tompkins. Adopted 2003.

Sandwich Boards and the Simmons Spoon

In 1949, a photograph that would become famous showed Simmons streaking across a stunning Malibu wave. "He was riding a foam core, veneer laminated, dual-fin concave," explained Elwell. "The picture is historic for the reasons of his early position and increased angle across the wave. His wake is long and flat, indicating great power and speed for slow Malibu."

Simmons' board was the answer. In the search for light weight, he considered making hollow Styrofoam boards, sort of a twist on the old Tom Blake kookboxes. Instead, he went modern. Styrofoam dissolved on contact with catalyzed resin, so the two together turned out to be impractical. Simmons made it all work by sandwiching the Styrofoam in between plywood, then glassing the whole thing over.

In late 1949, Simmons wrote to Quigg in Hawai'i, saying he had a board that weighed just 25 pounds. Simmons sold around 100 boards in summer 1949, opening a surf shop in Santa Monica to satisfy demand. "In those first days," Quigg said on the Legendary Surfers website, "Simmons would glue the plywood, Styrofoam, and balsa parts together, then Matt [Kivlin] would shape the balsa rails and glass them over." The business got too big for Simmons and Kivlin—who both wanted to surf, too—so they lured Quigg back from Hawai'i as a third hand. Quigg and Kivlin set up a separate glassing and finishing shop.

Three good heads coming together soon created better surfboards for the masses. Malcolm Gault-Williams explained: "As an example, Quigg fashioned the first fiberglass fin during this period and made further board innovations of his own. All three

CUSTOM SURFBOARDS BY

VELZY

The World's Largest Manufacturer

There are two types of materials that all modern surfboards are being made from. The first is a lightweight imported balsa wood and the other is a new scientific discovery called "polyurethane foam"; a lightweight, waterproof plastic foam substance.

The balsa boards are made from the finest kiln dried balsa wood, imported from Ecuador. Pieces of wood the proper length and width are selected for each individual board. The long strips of balsa are glued together with a strong waterproof glue while being subject to pressure in a specially designed glue press. The glued "blocks" are bandsawed to a rough shape specified by the customer. The "blocks" are next placed in a unique

"routing machine" that cuts the desired curvature of the deck and bottom. The rest of the shaping is done by hand. Skilled craftsmen finish each board in a manner desired by the customer.

The completed balsa boards are very fragile so they are given a tough coating of laminated fiberglass. The fin is attached and another gleaming Velzy Surfboard is ready for the water.

The "polyurethane foam" surfboards are handled in much the same manner. The plasic foam is first formed in a specially built high pressure mold, from there the foam "blanks" go through a process of shaping similar to the balsa wood surfboards.

LOCATIONS

and now...

4821 PACIFIC AVE. VENICE, CALIF. EXbrook 99095

1315 N. EL CAMINO REAL SAN CLEMENTE, CALIF. HYacinth 25525

MIDWAY & FRONTIER SAN DIEGO, CALIF.

scooped their noses, dropped the rails, and shaped tail blocks in various experimental ways. Simmons' boards were really wide in the tail. He wanted to get up and go! With concave bottoms and all those things he put back there, they did go. They went fast, straight across the wave. But, boy, the wide tail would push the nose down because the tail would ride so well. The scoop of the nose, concave bottom, and wide tail—it all worked. The boards had their problems, but the concept itself worked."

Their masterpiece may have been the Simmons "Spoon," a 10-foot-long solid balsa board with a full belly, kicked-up nose, thin rails, and a glassed and foiled wooden fin. With its pointed nose, Simmons likely developed the Spoon for big breaks like Ventura Overhead and La Jolla's Bird Rock, said Gault-Williams. Rennie Yater noted on the Legendary Surfers website, "His spoon nose, you know—it's

been copied ever since. It just made surf-boards—instead of being straight, with a little curve to them—quite a bit more curve to them. They didn't get essentially that way right away. He did, like I say, very extreme things."

There was a lot of experimentation in the Simmons salon at the end of the 1940s. Quigg brought back Hot Curl ideas from Hawai'i and applied the design to California surf. Dave Rochlen began building boards and was one of the first to experiment with color. Quigg remembered on www.legendarysurfers.com, "I used to play around with tints to make the boards look a little bit different, but Dave was the first person I recall who began applying modern-style, colorful designs onto surfboards."

Simmons' reputation was such that he became a victim of his own popularity: "At one time," recalled Greg Noll in *Da Bull: Life Over the Edge*, "Simmons' boards were in such demand that the pressure of meeting orders almost became too much for him. Like most of us, he really just wanted to surf. I remember once, he had something like thirty-four boards on back-order. Velzy and I both had had a Simmons board on back-order for three months. Simmons wouldn't answer his phone, so Velzy decided that we would check out the situation in person. Going to Simmons' shop was just as much an experience as riding one of his boards. The shop was on a

side street in Venice Beach. It was an absolute goddamn mess. He never cleaned up the balsa-wood shavings, so you'd have to make a path through the shavings and other debris to get from one place in the shop to another. Velzy and I arrived there about five o'clock one afternoon. The place looked all shut down. We pounded on the door. No reply. Velzy noticed that the door wasn't locked, so he opened it and called, 'Simmons?' No reply. We walked in cautiously through the shavings, calling, 'Simmons, where are you?' Finally, we heard a gruff voice from a corner: 'Whaddaya want?' We followed the voice and found Simmons sitting in the corner in shadow. He was eating beans out of a can, using a big balsa-wood shaving for a spoon. Simmons was eccentric. When he'd worn holes through the soles of his shoes, he'd cut a piece of plywood and tape it onto his shoe. With his perpetually uncombed hair, skinny physique and gimpy arm, he truly looked like a mad scientist. He didn't like many people, but he liked Velzy better than most because Velzy rode Simmons' boards and he rode them well. Besides that, he just liked Velzy."

Velzy Opens Shop

As the 1940s were ending, Dale Velzy was twenty-four years old and had been having one rip-snorting good time since World War II. Red-hot women, ice-cold beer, sharp-dressed man, hot rods, motorcycles. Velzy

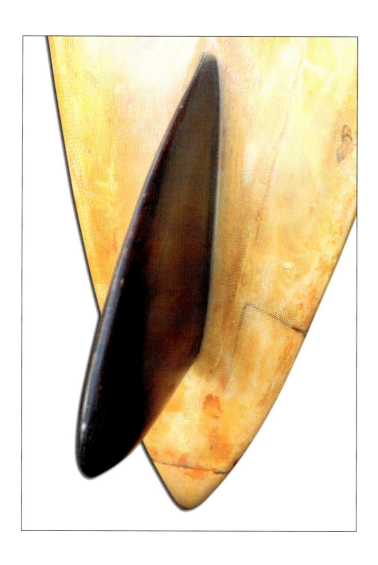

Luis Hangca Balsa Gun, 9'0"

Dating from 1954, this was an incredible gun outline for the era. It was surfed by Luis Hangca on the North Shore during the 1950s. Hangca was a member of the Hawaiian Team attending the surfing exhibition at the lifeguard demonstration in the 1956 Olympics in Australia. This exhibition also featured the introduction of the "Malibu" longboards by Greg Noll and Tommy Zahn. Adopted 2003.

had a booming business making, repairing, and reshaping boards under the Manhattan Beach Pier, but the authorities were getting on him. Again. So in 1949, Velzy borrowed some money from the uncle of a friend's wife, rented a small former shoe repair shop half a block from the Manhattan Pier, printed up a little sticker that read "Designed by Velzy," and unwittingly became California's first officially recognized surfboard maker. He had been visited by a city official who insisted Velzy get a business license and state resale number.

Surfboards by Velzy was an instant success. His shop became a hangout and business boomed. His rent was $45 a month and he was selling as many as ten boards a week at $55 apiece. Most of the boards Velzy was shaping had balsa cores, glassed by Bev Morgan. Velzy was experimenting with Hot Curls, but that design didn't really work in California's conditions.

Resin and fiberglass were easier to use than varnish, but the chemicals at the time were still sketchy. They had to be sun cured, and that could be a problem when the fog came in, wind came up, or sand blew across the beach and into a new glass job.

Fiberglass sealed the balsa, eliminating the need for redwood stringers and nose and tail blocks for all but the most hardcore old-schoolers. The raw materials cost for balsa was $18, while a plank cost $35 to $40, so it was cheaper to start from scratch with balsa than cut down a used plank.

As more people got involved with surfing and surfers got better in general and new surf spots opened up, the demand for a variety of boards to suit a variety of conditions and ability levels increased. The standardized Blake hollow boards and the Pacific System Homes models weren't cut-ting it anymore. The seeds of the custom surfboard business were being sown.

The World's Largest Surfboard Manufacturer

For whatever reason—and he probably had a few—Simmons closed down his operation after summer 1949 and moved to the family ranch in Norwalk. Too far out in the sticks for anyone to bother peaking and poking, Simmons delved farther to develop boards that were shorter, faster, lighter. "The best and last of a series of boards were made," wrote John Elwell. "The most notable were the double slotted, to improve paddling. Some very short ones appeared from six to eight feet of which examples still exist. He experimented with different tail dimensions. Stock models were quite different than his 'personals.' His own boards always had dual shallow fins and harder 60/40 rails, all the way down to 80/20. There was a huge vacuum left when Simmons quit producing boards. The summer of 1950, the modified copies came out. We asked him about that. He said, 'They are easy to make. Changing the nose and tails somewhat don't make that much difference. The nose sticks out of the water when we surf. I'd hate to get stabbed by a pointed one! If the tail is less than ten inches, it's a paddleboard! My noses are much more functional and stronger. The points break off too easy!'"

The productive Simmons-Kivlin-Quigg triumvirate had come to a quick end. Kivlin and Quigg soldiered along on their own. "Joe always made boards that rode better. They were much easier to ride. He wouldn't be as radical as Bob," Renny Yater said on the Legendary Surfers website. "Kivlin's boards were even quite a bit different. His style of surfing—you ever seen in the

Continued on page 106

Gettin' Piggy With It

Check out Dale Velzy in 1956, cruising up PCH to go surf The Malibu, living California's Golden Years of the 1950s as well as any man, setting the pace for surfer style to come. It is 1956 and Velzy is 29 years old, a sharp-dressed man cruising down the highway in a yellow 1955 Ford F-100 pickup truck. Outside is clean, inside is hot rod—power coming from a dropped-in V-8 Ford. Driving PCH listening to country swing or cowboy music on the AM radio, in the back is his secret weapon. The Pig.

Velzy is bad, he's nationwide. All over California, America, and the world, thousands and tens of thousands of surfers are riding Velzy Pigs and they are digging the new kind of surfing the Pig allows. The success of the Pig is powering Velzy's trip as he drives to The

(continued next page)

Dale Velzy Pig, 9'0"

Malibu. He is going surfing, to rinse away the sweat and grime of the shaping room and wash away the work and worry of being the "largest surfboard manufacturer in the world." There is a south swell running in from far away. Topanga is firing with only a few Valley Cowboys in the water, but Velzy is pushing on for the Bu, because he knows it's going to be cranking. Velzy will take his spot at the top of the point with all the usual suspects—Aaberg, Dora, Muñoz.

In modern terms, calling a surfboard a Pig is like calling a sports car a Turtle or a power-boat a Whale. To most surfers, a Pig is a slow, thick surfboard that doesn't work. But in the mid 1950s, the Pig was the most popular surfboard in California, and it was one of the first branded surfboards to go big: "You know how our most famous design came to be?" Hap Jacobs was quoted on www.legendarysurfers.com. "In the balsa days, there was a lot of sawing involved and Velzy wished we could just leave the tails blocky to save the trouble. Well on one board, he just left the tail fatter than anything and had her glassed. When he saw the finished board, he shook his head and said, 'Well it looks like the ass end of a pig.' Muñoz tried the thing out at the pier, and it went great."

Watch surfing footage of guys at Malibu in the early 1950s and you will see surfers like Joe Quigg shooting the curl at a fast angle and doing pretty aggressive cutbacks on boards that had a lot of belly and hopped up and down a lot, as if the boards had neurological problems. The Pig solved all that. Pigs were balsa, because Velzy loved working with balsa. A typical model was 9 feet, 6 inches long, 21 1/2 inches wide, and 2 1/2 inches thick. Nothing special. But the big difference with the Pig was that the wide point was on the tail side of center. The boards looked big in the hips, but that width toward the tail was just what the doctor ordered for a new generation of surfers who were surfing the tail more and more, and needed speed and drive out of their turns.

The Pig put the pork in hotdog surfing, and the results were both instantaneous and everlasting. To this day, the Pig is considered one of the most important surfboard designs of all time, for the surfing it allowed in the second half of the 1950s, and even into the mid 1960s. When Nat Young won the 1966 World Contest on Sam—a board that ushered in the shortboard revolution and all but killed the longboard—the design was a direct tribute to Velzy's Pig.

But let's get back to Velzy, cruising PCH in his hot-rodded truck, heading for Malibu where almost all surfers great and small are riding a Pig, or wish they were. Velzy is a few years away from moving up to his gullwing Mercedes 300 SL—and a couple more years away from losing it all to the IRS. But in the summer of 1956, he is on top of the world, changing the surfing universe and going to surf a perfect day at Malibu. When Velzy was asked in 2004 if it was all as good as it sounded, he replied, "It was better."

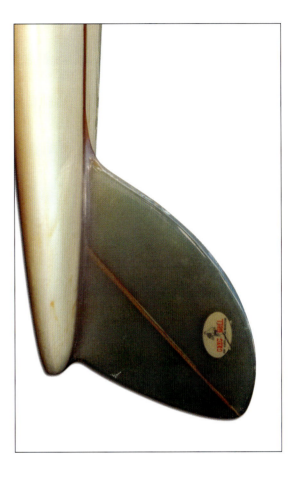

Greg Noll Longboard, 9'2"

This late-1950s longboard features an early and rare Noll camera-man logo. The board remains in nice, original condition. Adopted 1998.

Greg Noll, 1960s

Greg stands tall alongside his trusty 11'4" "elephant gun" as he sizes up the Pipeline shorebreak.
Photograph © John Severson

Continued from page 102

museum, the real thin 90 rails? Boy, he could really ride 'em, too. Really good. So, he just went off and did his own thing. You know, Kivlin and Simmons didn't like each other, either. But that was the admiration part of it, too."

By 1955, there was a demand for surfboards that kept the likes of Quigg, Kivlin, Velzy, and a handful of other shapers "working in fiberglass up to our armpits," as fellow shaper Phil Edwards remembered on www.legendarysurfers.com. "Between all of us, we had ruined the inside of more garages up and down the California coast than anybody."

In Hermosa Beach, the grom named Bing Copeland opened a shop along the beachfront. Rick Stoner opened Rick's soon after, just down the block. In Hawai'i, Henry Kaiser had launched his Hawaiian

surfboard industry was about to explode. He hired a manager for the Venice shop, appointed Del Cannon and Bobby Patterson to set up a factory and retail outlet in La Jolla, and hired Dewey Weber to run another retail shop in Hermosa Beach, a few blocks from Jacobs. In 1959, Velzy's business cards claimed he was the "world's largest manufacturer" in the surfboard industry. That was probably true, but not for long.

Hobie Sees the Future

Hobart "Hobie" Alter was just a Laguna Beach high-schooler when he began shaping boards in his father's garage. "I started out making maybe 20 boards a summer for my friends," Hobie recalled on www.legendarysurfers.com, "and it sure beat being a lifeguard. About the end of junior college—which took me a little longer because I was doing a lot of surfing and skiing—my father decided I'd learned everything I could, and he recommended I go into the board business full time." Hobie made 99 boards in his garage but saved number 100 until he opened his first shop at Dana Point in 1953. His production soared to 1,580 balsas, all but two of them hand-shaped by Hobie himself.

With typical precision, Hobie can pinpoint the exact day that he foresaw the transition to polyurethane foam. "One Friday night in February of '54," Hobie was quoted on the Legendary Surfers website, "this guy, Kent Doolittle, walked into the shop and showed us this little piece of foam that was about this big around and about that thick (Hobie's hands abstract a shape roughly the size of a deck of cards.) It was kind of crude, but it was hard and dense. . . . You could just get your fingernail in it. I was impressed.

Village on Waikiki beach and put in an order for 500 boards that was downgraded to 250, but that was still a big order even for a producer like Dale Velzy, who opened a shop in San Clemente and hired a platoon of guys to produce the boards, which were all colored pink.

Meanwhile, at the Venice Beach Surfboards by Velzy shop, Hap Jacobs reconsidered his partnership with Velzy and decided to break the bond and go off on his own. Velzy just kept on cruising along, most likely sensing the rumbling

At this time, when you said foam you meant what we call Styrofoam, which was horrible; you could take your finger and just push it right through. I mean, worse than a cheap beer cooler. Just huge, open-celled foam, like the kind you find in arts and crafts stores. We'd actually tried that stuff before. Renny Yater (who worked for me at the time) and I had each made one. I think Renny's turned out better, but they were both terrible. . . . They rattled like peas in a pod. You had to finish them with glue or epoxy. Joey Cabell actually loved the things; he rode one of them for a while. But they were no good, and we didn't pursue foam anymore. But Doolittle claimed that polyester resin wouldn't dissolve his little block of foam, so we tested it out. So I put resin on it. I put acetone on it. I glassed it . . . and that night I took that little block to a party, pulled it out of my pocket, and said, 'This is it, boys, the future of surfboards right here.'"

The major advantage of polyurethane foam over polystyrene Styrofoam was that polyurethane did not melt when coated with fiberglass and resin. This eliminated the need for any hardwoods, except for thin strips in the stringer.

Foreseeing the future and making it happen were two different things, however. Working with foam was a black art and not a science at the time. As Phil Edwards wrote in his 1967 book *You Should Have Been Here an Hour Ago*, Hobie "had seen polyurethane foam before, and one day he stood looking deeply into a cup of the stuff. He saw that (1) its ratio of strength to weight was enormous and (2) that it wouldn't soak up water like balsa wood. 'Surfboard!' mumbled Hobie, and took his cup to a chemical company. 'Dandy,' they said, 'except that you can't control the stuff in the size you want. This cup is about as far as you go, kid.' So Hobie did exactly what they told him not to do. He built a mold for the foam—roughly the size of a surfboard—and poured in a batch. He blew out the side of the garage: 'So much for the expansion properties of this junk,' he muttered. Of course, there was a little trouble with his father about the garage. . . . Hobie built a stronger mold and poured in another batch. He blew up the mold. He built more; blew them apart. . . . He constructed some molds of plaster of Paris and added a touch of concrete. And Gordon Clark—who had been to engineering school and knew all the right equations—began to work along with Hobie, figuring out the principles of molds and mixtures of foam."

Hobie was right about foam, but he wasn't the only California board builder who saw the future of surfboards in plastics. While most of the innovation in foam was taking place in Los Angeles County, Lorrin Harrison in Capistrano Beach, Orange County, is credited as the first to experiment with polyurethane foam in 1955. And Dave Sweet, who had earlier tried and failed with polystyrene Styrofoam, was now hot onto polyurethane foam. He told *The Surfer's Journal*: "For financial reasons, I went into partnership with a company called Techniform, and we built the [first full-sized] mold together and it cost me about $12,000. This was in a shop on Balboa Boulevard in Van Nuys. For a year and a half we kept pouring, pouring, and pouring. . . . No good. No good. And Techniform gave up; they said, 'Take that damn mold and get it out of here!' Then I got on the phone with all these chemical engineers from Rykold. I was desperate! I had the mold, but I couldn't make a good blank."

Greg Noll "Jose Angel" Gun, 11'8"

Hand-shaped by Greg Noll, this gun was crafted using a blank made of hand-selected balsa. It's a modern re-creation of the gun he shaped in the late 1950s for big-wave pioneer Jose Angel of Hawai'i. Adopted 1998.

Sweet became the first to make a commercial polyurethane surfboard. Setting up in Santa Monica, he worked with his brother Roger for a while, with backing from actor Cliff Robertson (who would later star as the Great Kahoona in *Gidget*) as a partner in Robertson-Sweet surfboards. According to C. R. Stecyk, Sweet first showed off his work in public in May 1956: "Dave Sweet, an idiosyncratic designer, paddles out on an unassuming looking marbleized abstract pigmented opaque surfboard. Astute local observers notice the change in Dave's surfing style and closely examine the stick discovering it to be unbelievably light in weight. Offering no explanations, Dave leaves with the mysto-prototype board. Insiders realize that Sweet has mastered the foam process. Next week he will offer the first commercial polyurethane foam surfboard for sale. It will be two years before he has any competitors. Paradoxically, Sweet will never take public credit for his innovation."

Things were bubbling elsewhere, too. In 1959, Larry Gordon was a 19-year-old chemistry major who teamed up with Floyd Smith to make polyurethane blanks in Smith's garage in Pacific Beach. These experiments turned into the Gordon and Smith label, and they hired a stable of shapers that included Mike Hynson, Skip Frye, Rusty Priesendorfer, Steve Seebold, Hank Warner, and Mike Eaton, to name a few.

Still, the efforts of Harrison, Robertson-Sweet, Gordon and Smith, and others would soon be dwarfed by the machinations of Hobie and Grubby Clark.

During the summer of 1958, Hobie and Clark rented a sketchy shack hidden away

Pat Curren's Big-Wave Elephant Guns

Through the 1950s, California surfers were tribal groups. Small surf communities bubbled and cracked around surf spots, each one a kingdom unto itself. La Jolla is a place that has always attracted the wealthy, bright, and eccentric, and during the 1950s a surf clique developed around the surf spot at Windansea that would have a profound effect on surfing and surfboard design.

Pat Curren was originally from Mission Beach and didn't start surfing until 1950, at age eighteen. But he had the brains and skills and determination that surfing required back then, and before too long he was a regular at Windansea. As Curren recalled, "In the early 1950s, I moved to La Jolla and got really serious about it. At Wind 'n Sea, Buzzy Bent, Towny Cromwell, Buddy Hall, and the Eckstrom brothers were riding 10- to 11-foot planks. Buzzy was one of the first to ride the Quigg chip, a fiberglass and balsa surfboard 9 feet long, 22 to 23 inches wide, turned-down rails, trying to get a rocker with a pretty flat bottom."

The La Jolla guys were different. They had an edge. They were low-class guys who acted like upper-class guys, and vice versa. "To be a La Jolla surfer in the '50s," wrote Bruce Jenkins in *The Surfer's Journal*, "meant you never held back: in your drinking, your partying or especially your surfing, where the test of skill was a double-overhead day at Windansea. Nobody savored that life, or typified it more, than Patrick King Curren."

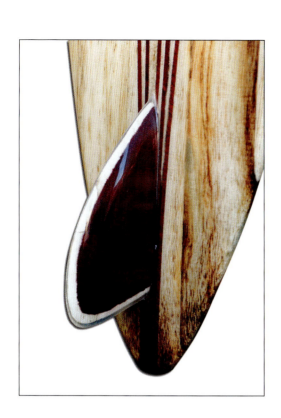

Pat Curren–Gary Linden Agave Gun, 10'11"

Gary Linden harvested the agave wood and made the blank for this board in the 1950s. Pat Curren then stepped in and did the shaping. The combined end result is a beautiful and rare redwood "fan" stringer. Adopted 2000.

Within five years of learning to surf, Curren was one of the first of the coast *haole* to charge serious Makaha and Sunset. In those days in Hawai'i, surfers scrounged a living as best they could—stealing chickens, diving for fish, living on almost nothing, and surfing, surfing, surfing. Curren's career as a surfboard shaper began as a bluff. "I started shaping boards in 1956–57," Curren said on www.legendarysurfers.com. "I was walking down the beach at Waikiki and a guy at a rental board place asked me who had made the board I was carrying. I said I did. He asked me to make twenty rental boards. So I rented a shop in Haleiwa and got into it."

(continued next page)

Curren had a short apprenticeship with Dale Velzy in California, but it was in Hawai'i where he learned to shape. Up until 1956, Makaha was the ultimate challenge for a surfer, a giant wave with a long wall that ended in a horrific bowl that would hold a surfer down and beat him like he owed money. At the time, life was all about taking off as far up the point as you dared, taking a high line, and making the Bowl, and that demanded a lot from a surfboard.

Big-wave surfboards earned the moniker "elephant guns," thanks to a statement by Buzzy Trent: "You don't go hunting elephant with a BB gun," said Trent. "If you're going to hunt big waves, take a big gun." During the mid-1950s, Curren was in the elite of the best big-wave surfers, a stoic, Gary Cooper kind of guy whose actions did all the talking. Curren lived for those big days at Makaha and he wanted to survive them, so he turned his cool self into the manufacture of what Mike Doyle called, "the most beautiful, streamlined surfboards any of us had ever seen. Each one of his boards was a cross between a work of art and a weapon, like some beautifully crafted spear. Curren had learned how to attach slabs of wood to the nose and tail of a board to get more rocker, or curve. And his boards went like rockets. In those days, speed was everything. Riding big waves wasn't about style or looking pretty or making graceful cutbacks or any of that. It was about going for the biggest wave and hoping you didn't get killed. Curren's boards were designed to go straight down the line, hard and fast. They gave you a chance at survival."

Doyle's words are supported by most of the big-wave surfers who put in hours at Makaha and on the North Shore in the 1950s. "Pat was putting rocker in his boards, which really set him apart," Fred Van Dyke was quoted on the Legendary Surfers website. "If you needed a board in a day or two, he'd have it right there on your lawn, and he did all this with some really crude tools. If challenged, this guy could shape a redwood board with a draw knife."

Curren's "real genius," wrote Mike Doyle in *Morning Glass*, "was in that one strip of Masonite that recorded the rail curve of his rhino guns. Curren developed that template through years of big-wave riding, countless wipeouts, who knows how many scars and bruises, endless hours at a drafting table, plus an enormous amount of natural talent."

"A lot of people don't realize that Pat and [Mike] Diffenderfer were shaping way ahead of Dick Brewer," Peter Cole reminded. "Pat was the first guy to produce the ultimate gun. Joe Quigg and Bob Sheppard were making nice boards for all-around surfing, but Pat made the stiletto, specifically for Waimea, where you go from Point A to Point B on the biggest wave that comes through."

in Laguna Canyon and painted the windows black to deter spies. Now, they plotted to truly uncover the best way to use foam. "I made a half-surfboard mold, and we started experimenting," Hobie recalled on the Legendary Surfers website. "It was just a huge mess. No one had seen a block of foam as big as the ones we were trying to pour. Up until then, foam was just used for picture frames, ornaments, that kind of thing. What we came up with was a way to pour two halves of a surfboard, whereupon they'd have to be stringered and glued up. We did most of our experimentation in an old bellyboard mold. We'd get the chemicals from American Latex and other companies, and just go at it. This was June of 1958."

Some of the experimentation included stress-testing the new materials, and Phil Edwards remembers standing next to Hobie on a high cliff overlooking the sea as Hobie chucked one of the boards to see how it held up: "It had bounced on the rocks a few hundred feet below—but it wasn't in bad shape."

The foam boards could be molded and shaped to suit any length or width or rocker configuration, but there were problems. The boards had a tendency to expand in the sun and ended up looking like loaves of bread or cigars. Hobie fixed that by forming the molds under high pressure and making them more stable. The blown foam also ended up with large "air voids"—oversize air bubbles that hurt the structural integrity and strength of the boards. Hobie and Clark painstakingly popped all those air bubbles and filled them, but then the boards had to be colored to hide the problems.

Some of the blank halves came out of the molds too thin, so Hobie used 2-inch balsa stringers for width. Modern surfboard collectors now prize these models with the thick stringers, as they date back almost to the beginning.

This was all serious business. Hobie hired off-duty firefighters to guard the shack because, as time went on, he and Clark were getting closer and closer to finding the secret sauce that would produce light, strong polyurethane foam blanks that would increase the production process exponentially. "My goal was to have a blank come out of the mold that had a crust on it, and then you'd just glass it," Hobie said on the Legendary Surfers website. "I was tired of shaping. I wanted this thing to be easy! But of course, it wasn't. We just couldn't get it to where it needed to be, so we ended up skinning 'em and shaping 'em, just like they do now. And, man, what a difference. After balsa, it was like shaping a stick of butter."

Hobie Alter and Grubby Clark are two of the men who put the "industry" in "surf industry." Contrary to the stereotype of surfers as beach bums, Hobie and Grubby were the Henry Fords of surfing—great businessmen, innovative thinkers, efficient producers, and decidedly unflaky entrepreneurs who sensed the wave that was about to break.

CHAPTER 6

Toes on the Nose, Feet on the Tail

Supplying the Surfing Sensation

1960–1967

WATCH OUT BRIGITTE... HERE COMES GIDGET!

COLUMBIA PICTURES presents

GIDGET

co-starring
SANDRA DEE · **CLIFF ROBERTSON** · **JAMES DARREN**

with
ARTHUR O'CONNELL · **MARY LaROCHE JO MORROW** and **THE FOUR PREPS**

Screenplay by GABRIELLE UPTON · Based on the novel by FREDERICK KOHNER
CINEMASCOPE Produced by LEWIS J. RACHMIL · Directed by PAUL WENDKOS **EASTMAN COLOR**

The joyous movie based on *that* book!

Before *Gidget*, surfing was the secret domain of a crew of just a happy few. After *Gidget*, a fuse had been lit that burned at flashpoint to ignite a surfing explosion.

In real life, Gidget was Kathy Kohner, a sixteen-year-old girl who learned to surf Malibu under the tutelage of a rasty crew of board bums who dug the Duke more than they liked Ike. But when her dad told her tale in the best-selling 1957 novel *Gidget* and then made the story into a 1959 movie starring Sandra Dee, the country went crazy for surfing. That first movie was followed by two sequels—1961's *Gidget Goes Hawaiian* and 1963's *Gidget Goes to Rome*—as well as a television series. By the dawn of the 1960s, the ancient Sport of Kings was a national fad and passion; as the Beach Boys were singing, everybody suddenly had an ocean all across the USA. And now, everyone wanted a surfboard.

In the film version of *Gidget*, one of those beach bums was a guy named Stinky who builds and repairs balsa surfboards on Malibu beach. "Stinky" was probably a play on "Grubby," as in Grubby Clark. Or maybe it was simply because surfboard mak-

***Gidget* Movie Poster, 1959**
Blame it on Gidget: *If all American literature derives from* Huckleberry Finn, *all American surf culture comes from* Gidget. *Columbia Pictures*

Opposite Page:
Popout Board, 8'10"
To supply the new surfing sensation, entrepreneurs sought to manufacture quick, easy, and inexpensive "popout" surfboards from molds.

Popout Board, 8'10"

*Most popouts were lamentable in the water, many
leaked and sank, and few survived. This early
1960s popout board boasted no stringer. It's in
excellent, unrestored condition—a true rarity.
Adopted 2003.*

ing has always been an itchy and scratchy business, and he was using fiberglass and resin and other toxic chemicals that raised a hellacious stink.

Inlanders, civilians, Valleys, and other assorted nonsurfers who watched *Gidget* saw Sandra Dee trying to huff a 40-pound balsa board down to the water's edge. They were thus likely fooled into believing that Stinky and the real-life cast of cool surfer cats were still riding hardwood boards in 1959—that is, if they had cared to notice. Truth is, by 1959 hardwoods had gone the way of jazz and the dodo bird and were already seen as Old School. Rock-'n'roll and plastics had taken over. The secret world of surfing was now out in full sunlight and had changed dramatically from 1957 to 1959. And it was about to change a whole lot faster.

While there were hundreds of converts to surfing every month, the happy few who had been involved in wave riding through the 1940s and 1950s stood aghast at the explosion of wannabes now clogging the lineup.

But where some saw apocalypse, others saw opportunity; some got lost, others got busy. The roaring wave of newcomers all needed boards. Following in *Gidget's* wake came a surge of demand that pushed production to undreamed-of levels at shaping shops such as Velzy–Jacobs, Hobie Alter, Dave Sweet, and Gordon and Smith, as well as promoting startups like Dewey Weber, Bing Copeland, and others. Within the next decade after *Gidget*, the surfboard was a new creature—yet again.

Going Electric

During the 1950s, filmmaker John Severson was making his own surfing movies. These weren't anything like *Gidget*; instead they were movies of surfers, for surfers. Along the way, he made a discovery, as he remembered: "One thing was immediately apparent. Surfers would devour any image of wave or surfer." In 1959, Severson produced a promotional magazine called *The Surfer* to launch his third surf movie, *Surf Fever*. He took most of the photos, did the illustrations and layout himself, sold some ads, and hoped for the best: "It was trying to be an art piece, really. But total surfing." It took Severson months to sell out, but he broke even. Despite the slow start, he published a second issue, and the next thing he knew, *The Surfer* became *Surfer Magazine*. Along the way, it also became the advertising platform for the surfboard wars that were about to begin.

One of the ads in the first issue of *The Surfer* was for Robertson-Sweet Surfboards—"Robertson" being Cliff Robertson, the La Jolla actor who had played the Great Kahoona in *Gidget* and wanted to get in on the ground floor of this surfing explosion he had sparked. Although the boards were advertised as "100 percent handcrafted," they were actually produced in a mold. The boards sold for just under $100 in sporting goods stores all around California—sporting goods stores because there were few surf shops at the time. By 1960, Velzy had passed from "the world's largest manufacturer of surfboards" to "the world's most troubled manufacturer." Revenuers from the state and federal governments were all over him and his shops in Venice, San Clemente, and San Diego. Velzy had hired surfer Dewey Weber to manage his Venice shop, but things soon soured. As Velzy's empire began to crumble around his ears, Weber took over the Venice shop, and Velzy never spoke to him again.

Weber was a live wire, both as a surfer and as a businessman. In the early 1960s, Harold Walker and Grubby Clark were the primary producers of surfboard blanks, and they were going full tilt to keep up with a demand that was mutating by the week—largely thanks to Weber. "He got the market going," Walker recalled on the Legendary Surfers website. "I had this van and every morning at 6 a.m. we loaded it up and off it went to Dewey's—60 blanks. We were running 24 hours a day then, with 25 to 30 guys working."

To try and cut down production time, Walker developed a milling and profile machine. "By the time we got a blank," Tak Kawahara recalled on the Legendary Surfers website, "it was milled and cut to

Mini-Malibu, 6'0"

Australian shaper Bill Wallace crafted this cool mini longboard. In the 1950s, Wallace was responsible for the Okinue hollow boards, basically using the 1930s technology of the paddle boards, but shaped as short longboards. Australian surfers christened these boards "Malibus." This board survives in fine, unrestored condition. Adopted 2005.

shape, with the sides squared off. We'd [just] finish it and turn the rails. Dewey . . . applied it and he advertised it. He had foresight. Surfboards were considered a piece of fine craftsmanship. Like fine furniture. Mention machinery and it wasn't considered soulful. It was like Bob Dylan walking on stage with an electric guitar [for the first time]. You've got to give him credit for thinking of the repercussions and using advertising to make it a positive."

And that surfboard demand continued to grow. By the end of 1962, more than 25,000 surfboards were sold in the United States annually, and a good chunk of them were Surfboards by Weber.

Wipe Outs

In summer 1962, a band of kids from Glendale, California, who called themselves the Surfaris got rides from their parents to a recording studio. Hoping to buy some new instruments—or maybe their own van—they recorded "Surfer Joe," a song that came to the drummer in a dream. Needing a B side for the single, they threw together an instrumental that used a speed-

ed-up high-school drum cadence with the world's simplest guitar line on top of it. They called it "Wipe Out." Within a year, the Surfaris were touring the world with the Beach Boys. By 2006, "Wipe Out" had been played on the radio 8 million times.

Not every surfer or shaper who had been involved through the 1950s was enthralled by the surfing sensation sweeping the nation. In Hawai'i, Pat Curren had built some of the finest big-wave boards, but by the 1960s he was starting to feel a little crowded.

Curren wasn't the only veteran of the golden years to get disgusted. On September 2, 1962, the final straw came for one of the primary surfboard innovators of the 1940s and 1950s. Matt Kivlin kicked out on his balsa streamliner for his last run at Malibu as a board surfer. He decided he shared little with the new generation of surfers, and after that last run, he parked his boards.

The irony of surfing is that the ocean is where a man goes to be alone with his thoughts, but that alone time was getting harder to come by as more men and women got into the lineups.

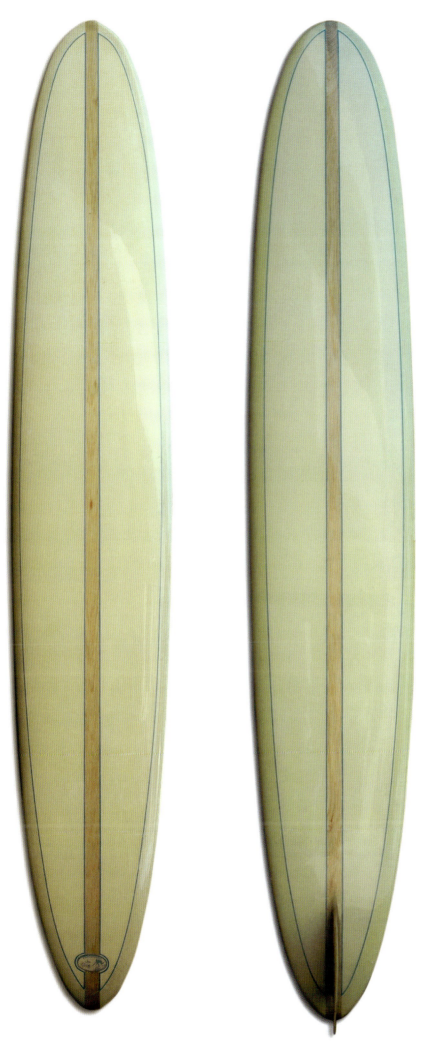

Joe Quigg Foam Paddleboard, 10'10"

In the early 1960s, Quigg made some twenty surfboard-class paddleboards. They were all under 11 feet and each had a surfboard fin. This board features a balsa stringer, with a Foss foam blank sealed and glassed with Volan cloth. The pale-blue pinlines were chosen to be the same color as the logo and high-density poured foam fin. The full-volume, flat-deck rocker was designed for paddling. Restored by Randy Rarick. Adopted 2005.

**Greg Noll
"Johnny Fain
Formula," 7'0"**
*Greg shaped this pintail
in the late 1960s. It's
fitted with a George
Greenough Stage IV
flex fin, still retaining
its original sticker.
Adopted 1999.*

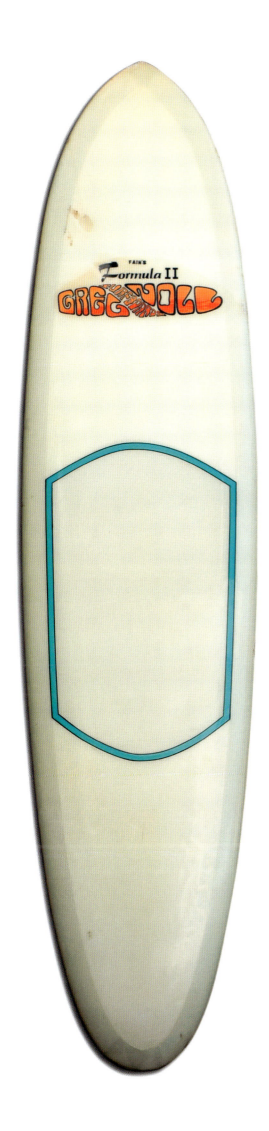

Greg Noll "Johnny Fain Formula II," 7'0"
Greg's Formula II model from the late 1960s featured a rounded pintail. It also bears a Greenough Stage IV flex fin. Adopted 2000.

Big Guns from Surfboards Hawaii

Just as Curren and Kivlin were packing up, Dick Brewer was arriving. Born in 1936 near Duluth, Minnesota, he was the son of an aircraft machinist, whose skills Brewer would inherit and put to good use. The family moved to Long Beach in 1939, and Brewer started surfing in his teens. His first board was a decrepit Velzy, but two years later he bought something custom: "I got my first custom board from Dick Barrymore . . . 9 feet long and 20 inches wide—because that's how long and wide the [balsa] wood was," Brewer told Drew Kampion for *The Surfer's Journal.* "It was a Woody Brown template, a double-ender he called 'em 'cuz the nose and tail looked the same. It'd be a semi-gun today . . . light balsa with single glass. It was lighter than my friend's Hobie foam board. I rode it for two years, up until I left for Hawaii. I rode everything in California on that 9-foot 26-pound balsa board—Lunada Bay, big Cotton's Point, Windansea, Ventura Overhead—so I knew you could ride a 15-foot wave on a 9-foot board."

In 1959, Brewer was going to Long Beach State, working as a die- and tool-maker and getting into hassles with unions because his age was behind his machinist skills. He was into hot cars and drag racing, but he was also president of the Alpha Sigma Chi fraternity. Back then the Red Scare was in full fear force and Armageddon was lurking around some corner; Brewer joined the Air National Guard but became disenchanted, fast: "They told me the Commies are gonna kill everybody who's anybody," Brewer recalled, "so I

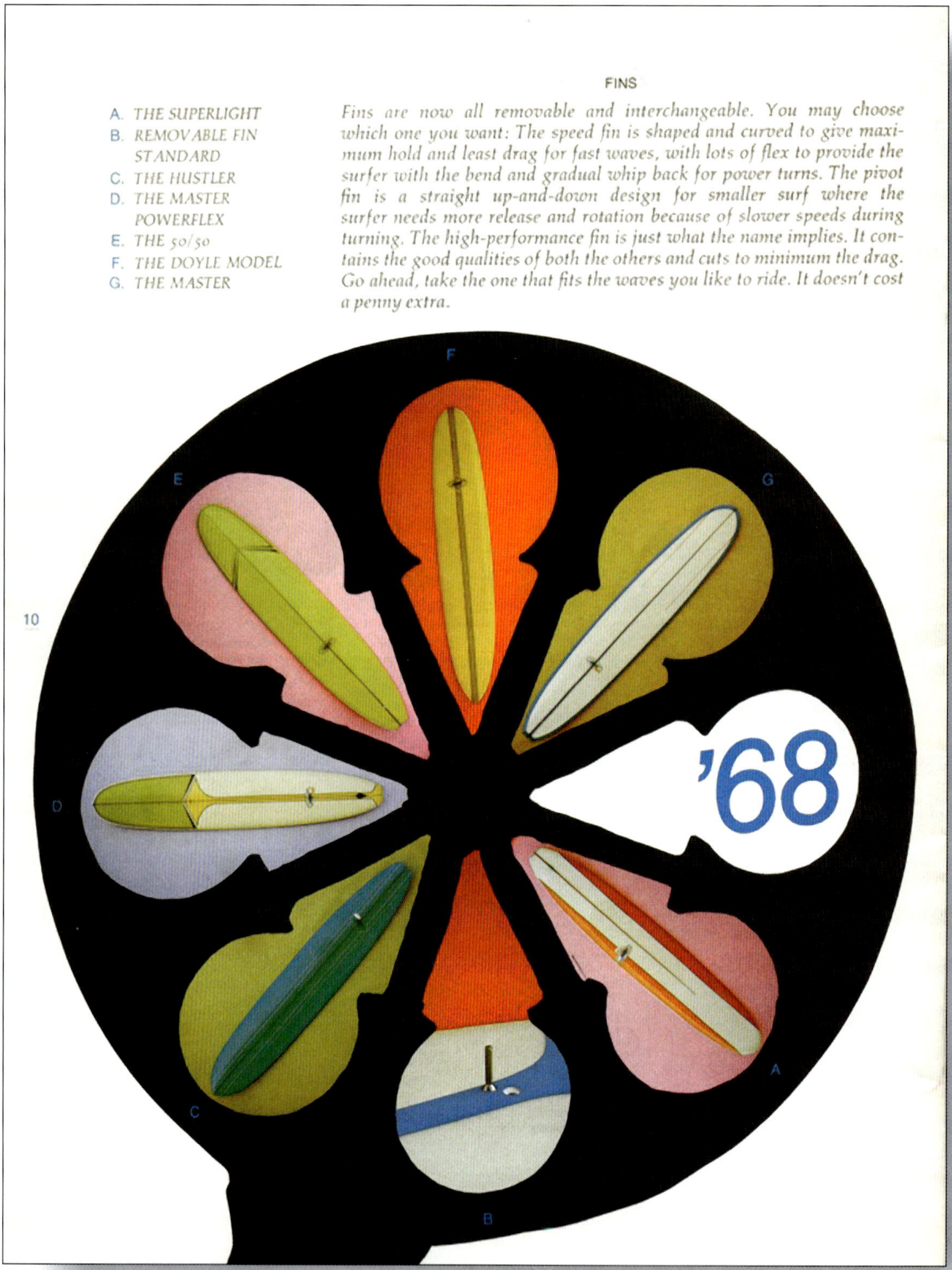

FINS

A. THE SUPERLIGHT
B. REMOVABLE FIN
   STANDARD
C. THE HUSTLER
D. THE MASTER
   POWERFLEX
E. THE 50/50
F. THE DOYLE MODEL
G. THE MASTER

Fins are now all removable and interchangeable. You may choose which one you want: The speed fin is shaped and curved to give maximum hold and least drag for fast waves, with lots of flex to provide the surfer with the bend and gradual whip back for power turns. The pivot fin is a straight up-and-down design for smaller surf where the surfer needs more release and rotation because of slower speeds during turning. The high-performance fin is just what the name implies. It contains the good qualities of both the others and cuts to minimum the drag. Go ahead, take the one that fits the waves you like to ride. It doesn't cost a penny extra.

10

'68

Hansen Surfboards Brochure, 1960s

surmised, 'Why be anybody? I'm just goin' surfing!'"

Brewer had worked on hot rods and dragsters; now, he turned his brain to the problem of water flowing under and around refined pieces of plastic. Brewer's first board was traced from a Joe Quigg template, using one of the first blanks by Harold Walker, who had started to blow foam in Newport Beach. Brewer made a 9-foot 10-inch gun in a garage in Surfside, took it to Hawai'i on his first trip there, and had a ball. He had just twenty units remaining for his engineering degree at Long Beach State, but surfing had him by the big toe. He returned to Hawai'i in summer 1960, and began to reshape the surfing world.

Brewer arrived in Waikiki armed with his homebrewed 9-foot 10-inch gun and a new 8-foot 6-inch Weber hotdogger, and at the time, that was a quiver: a smaller board for town and smaller days on the North Shore, and a trusty gun for the big stuff at Sunset Beach, Waimea Bay, Laniakea, and Makaha.

Now, Brewer figured he needed to get in the swing of Hawaiian ways, so he ordered from Curren a 9-foot-by-20-inch double-ender with dropped rails in the back for the North Shore. He arrived at the end of the Curren era, when Hawaiian surfers carried their elephant guns like lances: "A Pat Curren gun was ordered by how many feet of flat bottom you wanted—measured from the tail—and in front of that was a giant belly," Brewer told Drew Kampion. "So Diff [Mike Diffenderfer] says do 7 feet of flat bottom and we'll shape it together—perfectly straight and flat with dropped razor rails in back with the belly in front and a Pat Curren fin with about an 11-inch base, and when it was done, me and Diff and

Butch [van Artsdalen] were there, and Diff goes: 'Pat's got nothin' on us!'"

Brewer and Diffenderfer were challenging the established order. Curren and some of that established order had had their kicks, and there was about to be an immediate opening for someone who could make big-wave guns. Brewer was ambitious and he was talented, and he surfed hard at the big spots to establish his credibility as a big-wave surfer. During winter 1960–61, he opened Surfboards Hawaii in Haleiwa, at the west end of the Seven Mile Miracle on the North Shore of Oahu. These days there are as many as a dozen surf shops in Haleiwa, but Brewer's was the first. It must have been a lonely outpost back then, but less and less lonely every year.

At his shop, Brewer also sold surfboards imported from the mainland, from Dewey Weber and Scholl. And he shaped a few himself, under the wing of Bob Shepherd, and also influenced by Curren, who Brewer dared to question: "Pat Curren was an influence, too, because he was a friend, but his boards were so sticky, it turned me away," Brewer related to Drew Kampion. "The reputable part of Curren's trip was the razor rails and a dead-flat bottom, but I went into concaves with soft rails and a natural rocker." As Drew Kampion summed up Brewer: "When Brewer began to shape big guns, all that genetic material, that native instinct for mechanics and precision, began to translate into surfboards of distinctive craftsmanship and performance, even before he had much experience."

After Buffalo Keaulana won the 1961 Makaha contest on a Brewer board, others began asking for Surfboards Hawaii guns. As Brewer recalled, "Then I got an order for 50 Surfboards Hawaii a month from

Wigwam Department stores in Honolulu, and suddenly the Quonset hut I was living in became a factory at Kammieland [called Diff's Dumpers at the time]. Pat Curren, Jose Angell, and others had lived in the hut, so it had a history, but now Butch van Artsdalen, Mike Diffenderfer, Peewee (my glasser at Surfboards Hawaii), George Lanning, Mitch the Jew from Malibu . . . they all lived and worked there . . . and I was the only one that had a real bedroom! And that's how I really got started—that first 50 boards."

Selling the Surfing Sensation

In spring 1961, Hobie Alter and his buddy Dick Metz flew to Hawai'i on what was supposed to be a surfing safari—but became one of the founding flags of surf retail. As Metz recalled to Ben Marcus for a Surfing Heritage Foundation exhibit called Trunk It: "Hobie made boards and sold them out of the Dana Point store, but it really wasn't a store. It was just a garage where he made surfboards. And that opened in 1951 in Dana Point. So it was a surfboard shop like Velzy's with a room to display boards. In Honolulu, Hobie's agent was George Downing who was selling and renting boards off the beach at Waikiki, at Kuhio Beach. What Hobie got him to do— or what he was supposed to do—was write an order for a custom-made surfboard, send it to Hobie, Hobie would send the board back to George, and George would deliver the board to the guy. All production was here in California, and George got ten bucks for selling the board. Well, it didn't take Downing long to figure out if he started making the boards himself he could make more than ten bucks. So Hobie wasn't getting any orders, and we went over and Hobie decided to take over the dealership

from Downing. And he said to me—I wasn't planning on staying—he said, 'You've gotta stay over here and we're going to open a shop.' And I said, 'Hobie I don't know how to run a shop.' But I had had a liquor store and all that, so he figured I could figure it out. So I stayed and he went home and that's a whole 'nother story about the Hobie shops . . . I stayed over there and started selling surfboards."

At first Metz only sold surfboards, along with decals and patching kits. In California, the "Hobie Dana Point" T-shirts were hot with surfers and ho-dads, so Metz ordered a bunch of "Hobie Honolulu" T-shirts, which became even more popular, because even in the early 1960s it was still a big deal to go to Hawai'i: "That was the first clothing item we had in a retail store—and the store in Honolulu was the first purely retail store," Metz said to Marcus. "I bought the boards wholesale and marked them up and that's when the price of boards went from $85 to $100. Hobie could sell them to me for $80, and I could make 20 bucks for selling them. We were selling a lot of surfboards and it was really worth doing. We had racks of maybe twenty or thirty boards, and you could order a custom board for your height, your size, and your shape.

"But at the same time all this took off, all the other surfboard dealers—Weber, Bing, Greg Noll, Hansen, and G and S— they all wanted an outlet in Hawaii. I knew them all and they all wanted me to do it, but I couldn't because I was already the Hobie guy in Hawaii. When I realized they were going to get other guys to be my competition, I came over to the mainland to see Bing and Hansen and Weber and got their dealership. I went back to Honolulu and we opened a Surfline Hawaii retail store

Continued on page 132

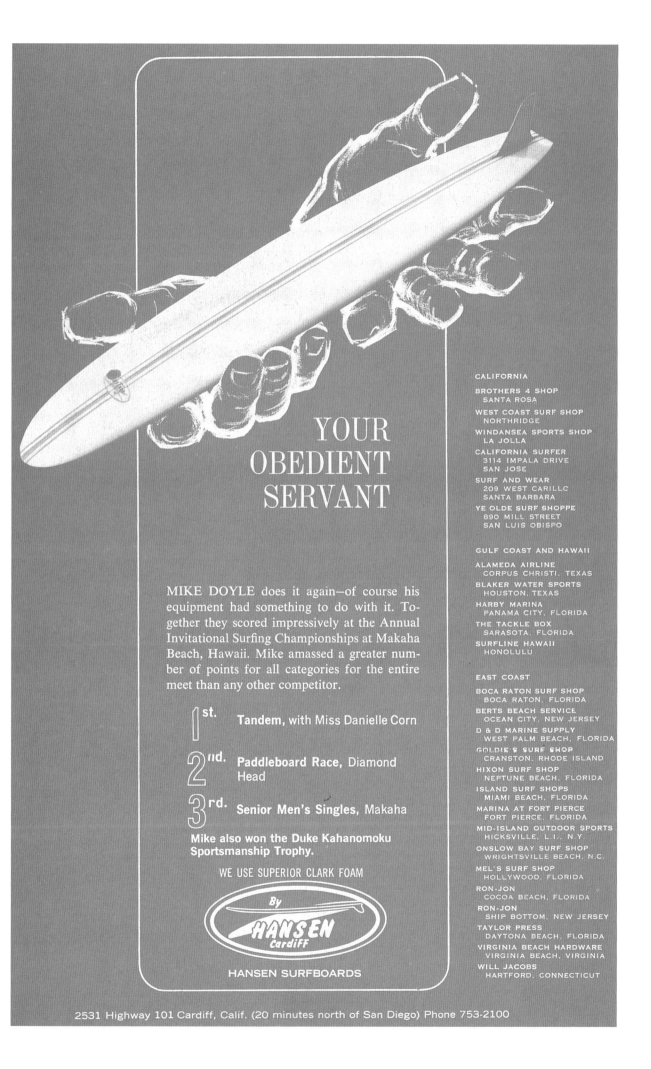

YOUR OBEDIENT SERVANT

MIKE DOYLE does it again—of course his equipment had something to do with it. Together they scored impressively at the Annual Invitational Surfing Championships at Makaha Beach, Hawaii. Mike amassed a greater number of points for all categories for the entire meet than any other competitor.

1st. **Tandem,** with Miss Danielle Corn

2nd. **Paddleboard Race,** Diamond Head

3rd. **Senior Men's Singles,** Makaha

Mike also won the Duke Kahanomoku Sportsmanship Trophy.

WE USE SUPERIOR CLARK FOAM

By
HANSEN
Cardiff

HANSEN SURFBOARDS

2531 Highway 101 Cardiff, Calif. (20 minutes north of San Diego) Phone 753-2100

CALIFORNIA

BROTHERS 4 SHOP
SANTA ROSA
WEST COAST SURF SHOP
NORTHRIDGE
WINDANSEA SPORTS SHOP
LA JOLLA
CALIFORNIA SURFER
3114 IMPALA DRIVE
SAN JOSE
SURF AND WEAR
209 WEST CARILLC
SANTA BARBARA
YE OLDE SURF SHOPPE
890 MILL STREET
SAN LUIS OBISPO

GULF COAST AND HAWAII

ALAMEDA AIRLINE
CORPUS CHRISTI, TEXAS
BLAKER WATER SPORTS
HOUSTON, TEXAS
HARBY MARINA
PANAMA CITY, FLORIDA
THE TACKLE BOX
SARASOTA, FLORIDA
SURFLINE HAWAII
HONOLULU

EAST COAST

BOCA RATON SURF SHOP
BOCA RATON, FLORIDA
BERTS BEACH SERVICE
OCEAN CITY, NEW JERSEY
D & D MARINE SUPPLY
WEST PALM BEACH, FLORIDA
GOLDIE'S SURF SHOP
CRANSTON, RHODE ISLAND
HIXON SURF SHOP
NEPTUNE BEACH, FLORIDA
ISLAND SURF SHOPS
MIAMI BEACH, FLORIDA
MARINA AT FORT PIERCE
FORT PIERCE, FLORIDA
MID-ISLAND OUTDOOR SPORTS
HICKSVILLE, L.I., N.Y.
ONSLOW BAY SURF SHOP
WRIGHTSVILLE BEACH, N.C.
MEL'S SURF SHOP
HOLLYWOOD, FLORIDA
RON-JON
COCOA BEACH, FLORIDA
RON-JON
SHIP BOTTOM, NEW JERSEY
TAYLOR PRESS
DAYTONA BEACH, FLORIDA
VIRGINIA BEACH HARDWARE
VIRGINIA BEACH, VIRGINIA
WILL JACOBS
HARTFORD, CONNECTICUT

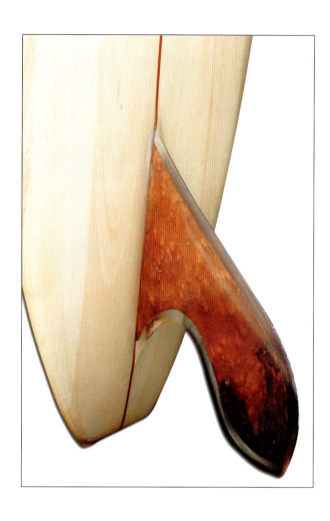

Greg Noll Balsa "Da Cat" #3, 9'8"

Shaped by Greg Noll, this Da Cat board was signed by both Greg and Miki Dora. The airbrushed image of Miki as the Red Baron originated from a mid-1960s image in Surfer *magazine. Adopted 2001.*

Hobie, 10'2"

A gloriously beautiful board made by Hobie in 1964. This was Butch Van Artsdalen's personal board, shaped by master shaper Mike Hynson. Butch rode this board at Pipeline and Sunset. Restored by Randy Rarick. Adopted 2001.

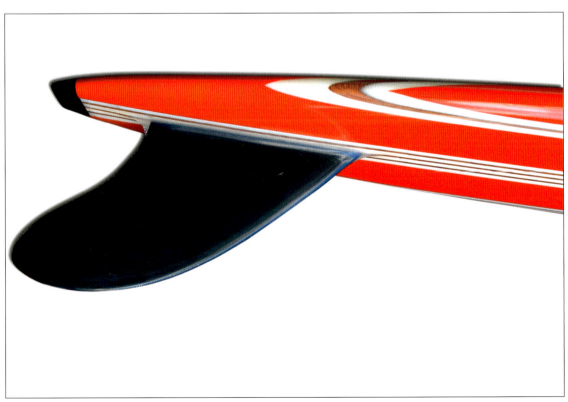

that then was the dealer for all the other surfboard makers. I was still with Hobie, but he didn't care as long as I sold only Hobies out of the Hobie store. Hobie knew that competition was going to happen, so it was better to have me own the competition than have the other guys be competing against me. This way I ran both stores, but no one knew I ran it, and I could compete with it better by owning it than not owning it."

Others were also entering the business. Joe Quigg came back to Newport Beach, after years of living and surfing in Hawai'i, and started shaping surfboards. Phil Edwards worked with him: "When I got hungry again . . . I went to Joe Quigg, who had a surfboard shop in Newport Beach, and who was one of the fathers of the lightweight board," Edwards wrote. "But more, Quigg also knew about boat-building, its technical and historical aspects. He was somebody special. Quigg made a boat that taught me a great deal. Further, he influenced all my present feelings about surfboards as well. As a bonus, I was making enough money to live on, say $25 a day—working only a couple of days a week and surfing and standing around looking at boats the rest of the time."

In the early 1960s, the Diwan company entered the "popout" market with a molded polyurethane foam and resin/fiberglass board. The firm started in a shop next to Bing Copeland's in Redondo Beach where a couple—Dick and Wanda, as in Diwan—were making molded fiberglass boats. They bought a board from Bing and made a mold out of it—all without Bing's knowledge, as he remembers today. After blowing about six or seven boards, the mold was expanded to have a round bottom and be about 1 inch thicker than Bing's original

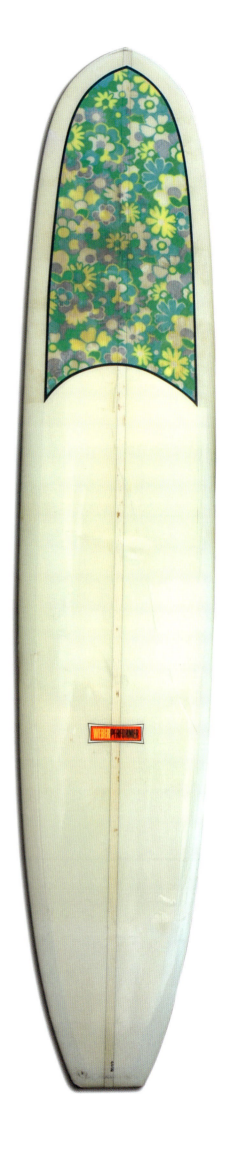

Dewey Weber Performer, 9'6"

Weber's Performer was one of the most popular boards of the 1960s. This survivor still bears its original SlipCheck and removable hatchet fin. Adopted 1998.

THE PERFORMER

Dewey Weber Surfboards proudly announces the addition of a new model to their line of surfboards. The "Performer" is the most versatile surfboard manufactured for the varying wave conditions of the coastal areas of the United States. This surfboard is available in two different designs, guaranteeing the rider of total performance and maneuverability in any type or size of surf. The Performer is not a "specialty" board like so many other surfboards on the market. It does not suffer any such limitations. The design of the performance shape differs from the "hot-dog" shape previously developed. It is not a modified semi-pig, but rather a parallel rail board. The shape was originally designed by Dewey for his own personal board. He wanted a surfboard to ride in surfing contests on the coast during the 1965 contest year. Since the wave conditions vary with each individual contest, the board had to respond equally as well in small or large surf, point surf or beach surf, and had to hold up under any type of conditions. Because the Performer has parallel rails it rides well in surf 1' to 8' and will not bounce or spin-out in the larger surf. The nose is fairly wide and is slightly rounded on the bottom. The wide, thin nose makes it possible to nose-ride in larger surf or surf as small as 1'. The rounded bottom near the nose plus the thinness of the nose, tail and rails provides maximum control while riding the nose. The special "turn" fin designed for the performance shape allows maximum turning potential. It is a deep square fin with an extremely narrow base. The narrow base of the fin eliminates the water pressure which causes drag when executing a turn. The turn fin enables the rider to accomplish a critical turn in surf as small as 1' when normally he wouldn't be able to. The fin also assists in maintaining stability in the soup on both large and small waves. The original performance shape handled so well in West Coast waves that Dewey felt by making slight variations in the shape a surfboard with the same outstanding features could be developed to suit the various surf conditions found throughout the Gulf area and the Eastern Seaboard. Such a board was designed and Dewey took it with him on his recent tour of these areas. The board was ridden by top surfers in every type of surf. Its total performance was outstanding. Thus, the performance shape was made available in two designs, The West Coast Performer and The East Coast Performer. The East Coast Performer is the first board designed and tested by a West Coast Manufacturer specifically to suit the needs of the Gulf and East Coast surfer. Stop in and see the new Performer.

DEWEY WEBER SURFBOARDS
DEPT. A, 4144 Lincoln Blvd. Venice, Calif. EX 8-0434

Al Beach Surf Shop
Tarzana, California

Hixon's Dewey Weber Surf Shop
Daytona Beach, Florida

Felix's Marina
Grand Haven, Michigan

Island Surf Shop
Sarasota, Florida

The Mogul Shop
Clifton, New Jersey

Monmouth Surf Shop
N. Long Branch, New Jersey

Ron Jon Surf Shop
Cocoa Beach, Florida

South Shore Surfer
Hull, Massachusetts

Tom and Ron Skin Diving Shop
Mobile, Alabama

Western Auto Assoc. Store
Virginia Beach, Virginia

Western Auto Assoc. Store
Burgaw, North Carolina

B.J.'s Surf Shop
Houston, Texas

Goldies Surf Shop
Cranston, Rhode Island

Hixon's Surf Shop
Neptune Beach, Florida

Jay's Surf Shop
Corpus Christi, Texas

Juno Surf Shop
Juno, Florida

Pleasure Point Surf Shop
Santa Cruz, California

Ron Jon Surf Shop
Ship Bottom, New Jersey

Surfline Hawaii Ltd.
Honolulu, Hawaii

Will Jacobs
Hartford, Connecticut

Ken Surf Shop
Galveston, Texas

Spyder Surf Shop
Ocean City, Maryland

board, but still with his template shape. Popouts would come and go over the next 40 years, but it wasn't until the twenty-first century that Randy French and Surf Tech would get them right.

Riding the Wild Surf

In 1962, Columbia Pictures tried to recapture that wave of popularity it had ridden with *Gidget* by releasing its second wave-riding film, *Ride the Wild Surf*. The cast included stars Tab Hunter, Fabian, Peter Brown, Susan Hart, Barbara Eden, and James Mitchum as Eskimo. Included as well was big-wave surfer Greg Noll, who became one of the inadvertent stars. Noll was the real-life surfer who was filmed to make celluloid-surfer Mitchum look good. As Da Bull told *The Surfer's Journal*: "Hey, I was just out there surfing, you know, because it was good Waimea that season. . . . We rode a lot of fun Haleiwa and Sunset and 15- to 20-foot Waimea, and I caught so many waves in those black-and-white trunks, they created the Eskimo character and wrote him into the movie."

While guys like Matt Kivlin and Pat Curren didn't survive the transition from the 1950s into the 1960s, others—like Noll—thrived. Da Bull became a surfing Renaissance man. Not only was he the leader of the pack in giant surf at Waimea Bay and Makaha, he was also an efficient producer of surf movies, surf photos, and surfboards.

Tak Kawahara now operates CHP Surf Shop in Redondo Beach, but he was there when Noll jumped into the board market in the early 1960s: "I started out patching surf-boards, then worked my way up through laminating to shaping," Kawahara said. "Over the years, I worked for several different surfboard manufacturers, including Con Colburn, Dewey Weber, Hap Jacobs, and Greg Noll. I was fortunate to have been surrounded by many great shapers of that time and learned a lot from them. I shaped boards up until the early '70s. Back then, the typical surfboard factory was tiny and always dirty . . . full of foam dust and resin, which would build up on your clothes and shoes. Greg's big factory [built in 1963] was a state-of-the-art operation from start to finish. I remember thinking, when we first moved in, 'Everything is so new and clean!' Greg's office was plush, nicely carpeted with several tropical fish tanks. The first time I went into his office I was covered with foam dust and resin. I thought the least I could do was take off my shoes. This became a sort of tradition, to take off your shoes, Hawaiian-style, no matter who you were, before going into Greg's office. The Hawaiian style is a big part of Greg. In the early days, the best part about it was, when the surf was up, nobody was working."

Riding the Nose

Another surfer from the 1950s who embraced the boom of the 1960s was Tom Morey. Born in Detroit in 1935, Morey moved to Southern California with his family at the end of World War II. He started on a surf matt at 12, then stood up when his family moved to Santa Monica. Another smart guy who loved the brain sparkle surfing gave him, Morey studied mathematics at the University of Southern California and took a job at Douglas Aircraft.

In 1964, he left the corporate world and opened up a surfboard shop in Ventura

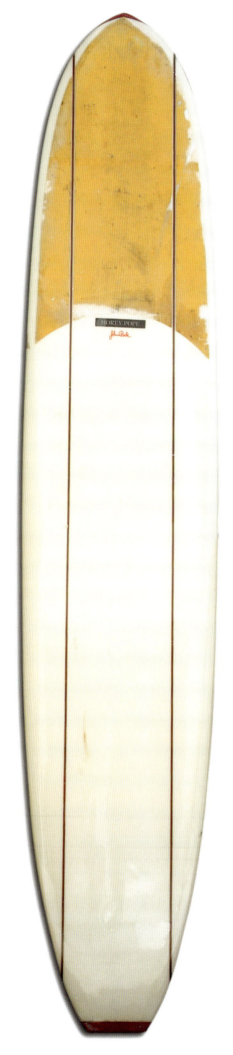

Morey–Pope Peck Penetrator, 9'7"
With its red fiberglass nose and tail blocks, offset stringers, and original yellow SlipCheck, this 1960s Penetrator was a super-fast ride. Adopted 1998.

with Carl Pope, which they called Morey-Pope. He also had a head full of ideas about edges and composite materials, and founded the Tom Morey Skeg Works. His first product was the first commercial interchangeable polypropylene fin system, baptized the TRAF ("fart" spelled backward). He also created Slip Check, an abrasive material in a spray can that you could spray on your board for traction, and the Tri Sec, a collapsible, three-part surfboard that folded into a suitcase. In 1965, his Skeg Works became Morey Surfboards. Mike Doyle—a 1960s surfer involved in everything from surf wax to funny hats to winning tandem championships and the 1968 Duke contest—remembered the engineering stoke radiating from Morey: "At that time the rails on all surfboards were rounded symmetrically, what we used to call 'egg rails,' and the nose always turned up so the board wouldn't pearl," Doyle was quoted on the Legendary Surfers website. "Well, on Tom's board the rails were turned down and were flat on the bottom, and the nose turned down as well. . . . At the time, I didn't really understand everything Tom was saying, but he definitely stretched my mind. We were used to making surfboards in the same old way, and if we experimented at all, it was more in the outline of the board, rather than with the rocker or the rails. And rather than working from theoretical concepts, we were still plodding along with trial and error, which was a lot of fun, but slow. We didn't even realize that nobody really knew how to design a surfboard. Tom Morey at least understood that when it came to surfboard design, the whole thing was still wide open. (And he was certainly correct about the turned-down rails, because that's the way all surfboards are made today.)."

To promote his surfboards, Morey organized the Tom Morey Invitational Nose Riding Championships on July 4, 1965, in Ventura. Yet because nothing like this had ever been done before, he struggled with the rules. "Weeks of stewing on how to promote my new little Morey Surfboards company in Ventura resulted in a pretty neat idea," Morey wrote in *The Surfer's Journal*. "Actually three ideas combined: hold a big surf contest in town and call it the Tom Morey Invitational, offer cash prizes, time nose riding rather than judge surfing. Cash might bring some unrecognized greats out of the woodwork, guys who wouldn't normally participate for trophies." This was the first-ever professional surfing contest to offer money, and it attracted some of the biggest names in small-wave hotdog surfing, including Billy Hamilton, John Peck, Johnny Fain, Robert August, David Nuuhiwa, and Corky Carroll. It also attracted some of the wildest surfboards of the time.

Morey did not like the subjective judging that clouded many surf contests, so the object of this exercise came down to beating the clock: The surfer who spent the most time on the nose of his surfboard, as judged by a stopwatch, would be deemed the winner. Morey's rules defined "nose" as "the front 25 percent of the board's length," and every competing board had to have that area marked out in paint. And that created problems, along with innovations.

Competitors began showing up the day before the contest for a little espionage. During warm-ups, Morey watched Dewey Weber having trouble riding waves on what was rumored to be a new-fangled contraption; when he wiped out, everyone got an eyeful of a fin with a turbo duct attached to the bottom: "Cripes, what if that something is an electric motor!" Morey recalled in *The Surfer's Journal*. "Would that ever be an idea! I sure didn't have such a feature as that covered in the rules!"

Mike Hynson and Skip Frye showed up with "two of the sweetest looking boards I've ever seen before or since," Morey wrote. "These babies were short (for their day), around 8 feet and with a lot of tail rocker. The noses were squared off and covered with rough nonskid 3M adhesive-backed boat decking. The traction must have been incredible."

Hynson and Mickey Muñoz battled it out in the final, Muñoz snagging a wave in the last few seconds to win by seven-tenths of a second. Many years later, Morey recalculated the score sheets, realized there was an error, and wrote a letter to Hynson saying there had been a miscarriage of judging and Hynson should have won. But it was in the history books.

Barefoot Iconoclast

As Hobie was setting up shop, Velzy was going down, Weber was taking over, and Brewer was on his way to Hawai'i, George Greenough was just getting out of high school and trying to decide what he wanted to do with himself. Born in 1941, Greenough was heir to a railroad fortune and raised in a Montecito mansion. Yet he wanted nothing of the ritzy life. It's possible that an early brush with death made him determined to live life however he wanted. While still a grade-schooler, Greenough had open-heart surgery. As his friend John Bradbury told *The Surfer's Journal*, "Maybe

Duke Kahanamoku, 9'6"

This stunning Hawaiian longboard was shaped in 1965. It features a redwood nose and tail block. Adopted 2001.

that's why he is the way he is, living every day to the limit. He's really one of a kind."

Greenough began surfing in the 1950s, with easy access to all the great Santa Barbara County point breaks from Hammonds Reef to the Hollister Ranch. And just as Greenough never cottoned to shoes, he also didn't like the standup surfboards of the time. So, he switched to knee-riding and mat-riding, in part because it put him closer to the wave. In high school in 1959, he used the school woodshop to make his first kneeboard from balsa. The board had an S shape to the deck and a rail line that ran from down in the back to up in front. According to Greenough in *The Surfer's Journal,* "It didn't have enough nose lift for bumpy conditions, but it flew in clean waves. Originally, it had a fin similar to what they were using on conventional stand-up boards at the time. I eventually designed the one you see here, which was the first flexible, high-aspect ratio fin I tried. It was based on a dolphin's dorsal fin, and it made an unbelievable improvement to the speed and handling of the board. The fin moved with the water flow, so it never cav-

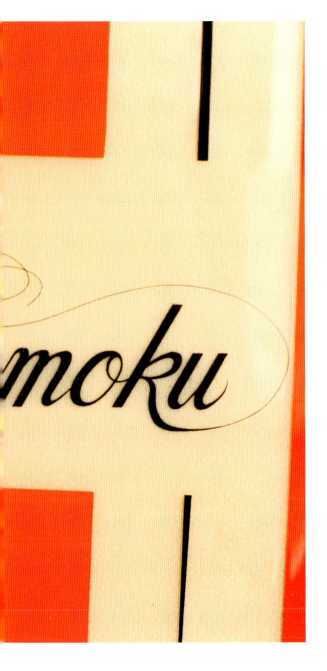

ground up. There was no consideration for anything like trimming or noseriding. It was made to power turn in the pocket. Like my balsa spoon, it started out as a twin fin, but ended up being a single fin. Single fins just suit displacement hulls better. After I rode the Baby Surfboard awhile, I scarfed some wood on the nose and added some lift. You can see that it had an extreme S curve to the deck, and that the rails were full and round all the way through the tail. The S deck got a lot of weight out of the nose, and the soft rails in the back let the wide tail bank over into a turn easier. It didn't have any vee in the tail."

While just about everyone else was hanging ten and walking the nose, Greenough created his breakthrough kneeboard, Velo, in 1965. Unlike anything that had gone before, Velo featured the distinctive "spoon" shape, which has been the trademark feature of Greenough's boards ever since.

Based on a performance concept Greenough called "neutral handling," the board was designed to flex in the same way his fins did. With a Bob Simmons-like plan shape that was buoyed only by a foam-filled rail section (the middle of the board was just fiberglass, tapering back to a flexible glass tail), the board just barely floated itself.

Still, Velo weighed only about 6 pounds and was powered by an 11-inch high-aspect fin designed and built by Greenough. Wide and thick at the base, then sweeping and tapering to a raked tip, the fiberglass foil loaded up on torque and propelled his kneeboard out of a turn with alarming force. Greenough was experimenting several decades ahead of his time: "I decided to try to make an entire board that flexed like my fin," Greenough told *The Surfer's Journal.*

itated or stuck in a track. The success of that first fin influenced everything I've designed since."

Out of high school, Greenough applied what he had learned on his kneeboard to a standup surfboard he called the Baby Surfboard: "I shaped the Baby Surfboard at the same time I made my first solid balsa spoon kneeboard," Greenough told *The Surfer's Journal.* "That was in 1962. The Baby Surfboard was 7 feet 8 inches by about 22 inches, and it had dead straight tail rocker and a fairly deep displacement hull. It was designed for shortboard surfing from the

"Fish moved when they swam, so why not make a whole board that moved when it rode waves? The difference between the solid balsa kneeboards with stiff fins and flexible fins was very noticeable, so the next step was to make an entire board that flexed in a similar manner. I used the balsa spoon as a male mold and laid up a fiberglass shell over it. Then I shaped some foam bones left over from a Yater semi-gun and laminated them into the outer rim of the shell and glassed over that. I tuned the whole thing with a grinder so it would progressively be more flexible towards the tail. Since it was the same shape as the board I had been riding for three years, I already had the fin set-up dialed in. Starting with a familiar shape was the perfect way to test the flexibility concept. The first flexy didn't go well on smaller waves, but if it was over 5 or 6 foot it just ripped. Plus it handled big, gnarly, bumpy waves with a lot more authority, because it could absorb the bumps as it moved over them.

"What made Velo such a challenge to ride was that it had untold gears. Because of its deep displacement hull, it never peaked out. No matter how fast you were going, you could bury the forward rail into a bottom turn and break the fin out, and it would jump into the next gear. The best that board ever worked was one day at a place called Moffet's in Australia. It's a reef break with gobs of power. It was 8 to 12 feet that day and offshore. There was so much power off the bottom, you couldn't kill it, no matter how hard you turned! A guy was watching me from on the beach, and he told me later that the board looked like a water ski when it turned. That's exactly how it felt!"

The Shape of Things to Come

When Greenough made a second trip to Australia in 1965, he had a fateful meeting

with a young up-and-coming surfer named Nat Young. "I didn't meet Nat until I was on my second trip to Australia in '65," remembered Greenough in *The Surfer's Journal*, "He was just unbelievable. Very powerful, very impressive. He had the strength to throw around longboards like they were shortboards. Plus, he had a good feel for where to put the board on a wave. He was riding boards just over 9 feet long, which was the same size board that guys who weighed 140 pounds were riding. Nat stood out in a way that nobody does today. There are so many good surfers nowadays who are so close in ability level, you can barely distinguish them from the beach. Nat was just miles ahead of everybody else at the time. He was riding longboards like they were shortboards, but he was also noseriding with a lot of sensitivity."

And Nat Young had a friend, a fellow surfer named Bob McTavish, who was starting to shape some boards. Young and McTavish were both influenced by that odd American, George Greenough. Together, they were the leading edge of the "Involvement School" of surfing, shunning traditional turning and nose-riding for a kind of surfing that was centered around the curl of the wave—turning up into it, flowing through it, and cutting back to get more. The idea was to "use the power part of the wave to maneuver really fast without any loss of speed," according to McTavish.

At the time, the average surfboard was around 9 feet 9 inches, weighed 25 pounds, and did not have the speed or performance that Young and McTavish wanted. They wanted to ride waves standing up with the same style that Greenough rode with on his knees. So, McTavish designed for Young a board christened "Sam"—a 9-foot 4-inch squaretail that was 2 1/2 inches thick with a swept-back fin crafted by Greenough.

Young traveled to California with his new secret weapon, and he and Sam got to know each other, surfing the points at Hollister Ranch, the same waves that had inspired Greenough's close-to-the-curl style of surfing. "He was riding Sam, which was 9 feet 4 inches and really thin," Greenough said. "Just a blade. We worked the fin over with a grinder and got it tuned up. He was unbeatable on that board."

For three weeks, Young got tuned up on Sam. Then he drove south to Ocean Beach to change the world.

The surfing world came together at Ocean Beach, San Diego, in fall 1966 for the third World Surfing Championships. It was the biggest surf contest ever held on the mainland, with 80,000 spectators. As Mike Doyle remembered, "At the time we were all riding 10-foot surfboards with trash-can noses, and we were still into an old-fashioned style of surfing where you stomp on the tail to kick the nose up, let the wave build-up go in front of you, then you either run forward and crouch down inside the tube, or else you stand on the nose and arch back in a kind of pose. We had all these stock poses we did over and

Nat Young, 1966

Many years of experimentation by American George Greenough and Australian Bob McTavish in the long, perfect points of California and Australia lead to the alchemy of a board some called Sam and others called Magic Sam. Shorter and lighter and narrower than the typical noseriding boards of the mid-1960s, Sam was the secret weapon of the Involvement school of surfing, and Nat rode the board to win the 1966 World Contest at Ocean Beach, San Diego. Photograph © Rob Stoner

over—el Spontaneo, Quasimodo, Nose Tweaking, Bell Ringing. They had originated back in the goofy Malibu days and had been a lot of fun over the years. But they had also stifled the creation of new styles. It was time to move on to other things."

In warm-ups, there were two schools in play. "The California cruise, best exemplified by the surfing of [David] Nuuhiwa and acolytes like Dru Harrison, used the surfboard as a platform for manoeuvres, some of them quite spectacular, like Nuuhiwa's ten second nose rides," wrote Australian journalist Phil Jarrat. "The Australian power style of Nat Young and Queensland surfer Peter Drouyn used the surfboard to attack the wave, riding in parts of it that had never before been utilized." Mike Doyle remembered Nat Young's board as "an old, beat-up, 9-foot log that looked like hell. But it was shaped like one of the old Pig boards—a shape that had mostly been forgotten. . . ." Little did he realize the shape of things to come.

Sam was a variation on Dale Velzy's Pig—whether accidentally or on purpose. But, whatever—it worked. "Then Nat Young, with his born-again Pig board, made a quantum leap in style," Doyle continued. "Instead of nose-riding like the rest of us, Nat was making lines and patterns on the faces of the waves. And that board of

his, which looked like a piece of junk to us, was really pretty sophisticated. Besides being small (9-foot was small to us then), it had a continuous-curve outline and continuous-curve rocker. While we were riding long straight cigar boards, Nat's board was much more suitable for doing cutbacks and what I call S-turn surfing."

Young impressed everyone who watched, including Hawaiian big-wave surfer Jeff Hakman, who would take the Involvement School out of the 1960s and into the 1970s and do beautiful things at Sunset Beach. As Hakman recalled, "Nat was cranking his board . . . and doing roundhouse cutbacks like I'd never seen before. He'd just drive it out onto the shoulder, plant those big feet of his on the rail, and wind it back in. [Peter] Drouyn used a lot of little turns to tuck into the best part of the wave all the time, very tight, very controlled. They were both riding the wave, not the board, and that made the difference."

"Nat gave us all a lesson in the future of surfing," Doyle testified. "While we would cut back or stomp on the tail to stall, Nat would cut back by compressing his body and pushing out with his legs, driving to get more power off his fin. He came out of a turn with more power than when he went into it, which allowed him to keep the board moving all the time, cutting a much

bigger pattern in the water. He would accelerate way out into the flat of the wave, cut way back into the curl, then drive way out in front again. The waves at Ocean Beach were small and mushy, but Nat was still carving all over them."

It was the big showdown between Old School and New School, noseriding against involvement, toes on the nose against feet on the tail, Australia against America. And yet the duel between the chief proponents—Nuuhiwa versus Young—didn't take place, as Nuuhiwa went down in an early heat, despite a 10-second noseride. "I was disappointed," said Nuuhiwa, talking about the fact he and Nat never got to duel it out, "because I came down with the flu after a good first day."

Nat Young emerged the winner, and surfing and the surfboard changed forever. As Hakman summed it up, "I think Nat's performance at San Diego in '66 really was a benchmark in world surfing. It was the last of the longboard contests, and seeing what Nat could do on a board that was basically a log, made us all realize what was possible if we had better equipment."

CHAPTER 7

You Say You Want a Revolution

From Sam to the Thruster

1966–1981

The Owl riding on Dick Brewer Wings

East Coast dealer:
Sunshine Surf & Sea
417 Main St.
Islip, Long Island, N.Y.
(516) 581-9212

CLARK FOAM

Dick Brewer Surfboards

1230 Kapiolani Blvd.
Honolulu, Hawaii 96814
106 Fifth St.
Huntington Beach, CA (714) 536-9100

After Nat Young and his shortboard named Sam upset the world at the 1966 World Surfing Championship, wave riding became very different very fast. The new "Involvement" school of surfing was suddenly everything to a tuned-in audience. The shortboard revolution had arrived.

In the aftermath of Young's ride, Young and surfer-shaper Bob McTavish went back into hiding in Australia—Nat a celebrity, McTavish back to his drawing board at Lennox Head. Meanwhile, the entire surf-industrial complex was thrown into a tizzy. For the first time—but hardly the last—everyone from blank makers like Grubby Clark and Harold Walker to teenaged surf-shop grommets changed the way they designed and produced and bought and sold and thought about surfboards. As Paul Gross wrote in *The Surfer's Journal*, "In an abrupt, eighteen month span between 1967 and 1969, virtually 100 percent of the active, worldwide surfing community abandoned longboarding in favor of the shortboard. To put that into perspective, imagine if everything you saw in the

**Dick Brewer
Surfboards Ad, 1974**

Opposite Page:
**Harbour Baby
Gun, 8'6"**
*This 1967 Baby Gun
dates from the height
of the pintail era.*

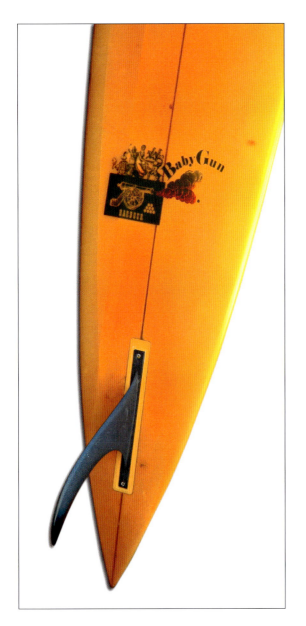

Harbour Baby Gun, 8'6"
This 1967 Baby Gun is fitted with an original WAVE fin system. Adopted 2003.

water today—shortboards, longboards, bodyboards, everything—was gone in two years, replaced by something you hadn't yet imagined."

Young's victory also turned up the heat on the rivalry between American and Australian surfers. And with that, the future of shorter surfboards fell into the hands of two men on opposite sides of the Pacific: In this corner, shaping for the Americans, was Dick Brewer; on the other corner of the Big Water, Bob McTavish was the Man, aided and abetted by

American semi-pat George Greenough. Over the next few years, these two sides would meet in swift collision all around the world, and that clash would forge the modern shortboard.

Dick Brewer's "Sword of Hercules"

Dick Brewer had been working with Hobie Alter, but now he went his own way. He spent summer 1966 making some 150 of the Trestle Special model for Rich Harbour: "The Trestle Special was a board I really believed in," Brewer told Mark Fragale of

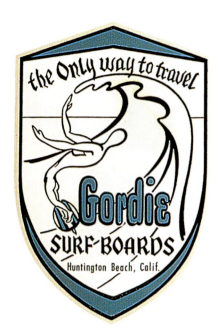

Longboard Magazine. "The rocker was correct in every detail, kicked in the nose and flowing evenly throughout. Just magical! They were relatively lightweight due to the decreased volume of the narrow template. The Trestle Special played a significant role in the way I fit my thinking into the eventual development of the Bing Pipeliner."

While at Harbour, Brewer worked with Steve Bigler on the Cheater model as well as crafting big-wave guns for Mark Martinson, Jock Sutherland, and Jackie Eberle. All through the summer, Brewer made it clear he would return to Hawai'i as the Pacific got ready to rumble.

In fall 1966, Copeland and his friend Duke Boyd—a Californian who founded the first major surfwear label, Hang Ten—flew to Maui to recruit Brewer to make surfboards for Bing. This was a smart business move, as Bing was dominant in California but needed credibility in Hawai'i. Bing foamed the runway by making a deal with Fred Schwartz, the owner of Surfline Hawaii and a Bing dealer, to provide space for Brewer to create. To further woo Brewer they presented him with a perfect, polished Skil 100 planer that gleamed like Excalibur. As Boyd explained, "There are two heroes in surfing—the surfer and the shaper. Together they pair off and work off one another. The deal with the shining planer was highly symbolic. Call it the 'Sword of Hercules' if you will. The planer is the shaper's sword to cut out the shape, the surfer's saber. The polished planer made that statement."

Bing began producing ads promoting Brewer as the first "star" shaper, placing him on a pedestal with the best surfers of the day—including David Nuuhiwa, who was riding for Bing. At Bing, Brewer found the time and money and support to do what he had wanted to do for Hobie: create a class of high-performance guns for Everysurfer.

While working for himself and for Hobie, Brewer had called some of his boards "Pipeliners." Now at Bing, the name stuck. As Mark Fragale wrote: "They all used roughly the same adjusted template, moving wide points fore and aft and changing foil and rail contours as the designs evolved. [Brewer] officially tagged the design 'Pipeliner' while at Bing's, the only exception being the few Buzzy Trent Model guns that he produced at Surfboards Hawaii. The Pipeliner was available in

Ben Aipa, 1980s

From the late 1960s and into the 1980s, Ben Aipa was one of the leaders of the modern hotdog surfing revolution. A great Hawaiian surfer, he nearly took out a couple of Duke events with his arm over the head as he rode out bottom turns. He experimented with wings and stingers and swallowtails for a hot crew of Hawaiian surfers that included Buttons Kaluhiokalani, Larry Bertlemann, and Mark Liddel, and those surfers went off under the "anything is possible" credo. This is Ben at Haleiwa, test driving one of his own models. Photograph © Jeff Divine
.

three models, all with their own identifying laminate: the Pipeliner (referred to as the 'Standard' or 'Pipeliner East' for units shipped to that region), the Island Semi, and the Island Gun. All models shared the same stringer design: a redwood center strip with offsets available in a choice of white or blue high-density foam or wood t-bands. This was a carry-over from his earlier design with Hobie, but the stringers were scaled down in width and material to reflect a growing desire for lighter weight surfboards."

Big-wave guns were still big and solid during winter 1966–1967, but the winning surfers were becoming smaller and so they asked for surfboards that were lighter, more refined, and more maneuverable. Greg Noll Surfboards likely ushered in lightweight foam blanks, leading the way for the industry. As Brewer told Drew Kampion, "Noll was blowing his own foam and was experimenting with lightweight densities. I recall seeing several examples of lightweight beachbreak boards that really stirred my imagination." Brewer's work during winter 1966–67 took in the work of Joe Quigg going back to the late 1940s, which was improved on by Pat Curren during the 1950s. But the Pipeliner was something new—a lighter, faster production big-wave gun for those thoroughly modern surfers.

Brewer met with Joey Cabell and Jeff Hakman, two of the new breed of lighter, sleeker big-wave surfers, and they were interested in surfboards that were as light and sleek as themselves. "Clark Foam (and Dick Morales, in particular) did a run of light foam for the Pipeliner and the Nuuhiwa Lightweight at the same time," Mark Fragale wrote. "To Brewer's best recollection, they may have driven the density of the foam into the 2.5 pound range, which proved too light for an

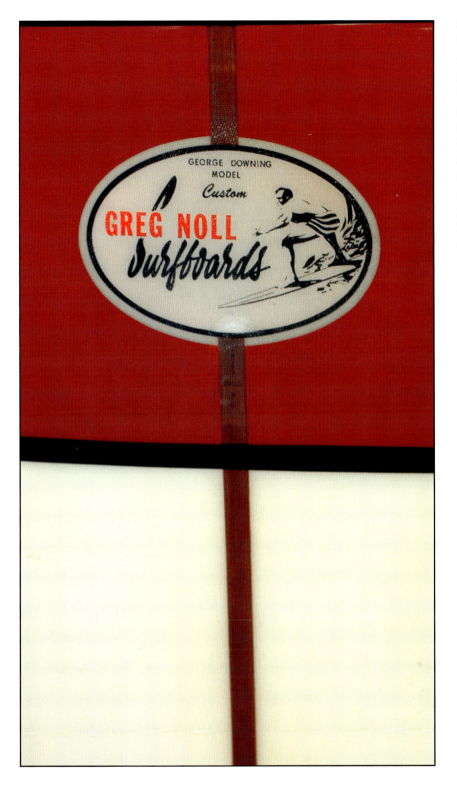

**Greg Noll
"George Downing
Model," 9'6"**

*Fewer than twelve of
these rare boards were
made in 1967. This is
one of only six known
to exist today, shaped
by Downing and built
at the Noll shop in
Honolulu. The board
featured an unique,
turned-down nose.
Adopted 2001.*

acceptable strength-to-weight ratio. They settled at a 3.0 pound density for the remainder of the Pipeliner run. The light-weight blanks featured a rocker design sporting a flat midsection with pronounced kick in the nose and tail. This became a vital part of Brewer's gun design criteria."

Those dialed in to what Young had accomplished at Ocean Beach knew that George Greenough's foiled fins were at the base of everything. Beginning in 1966, Greenough's Stage III and Stage IV were manufactured and heavily promoted by Morey-Pope. With the Stage III, noseriding was no longer the game; instead, full-on power turning was at the heart of the board's design. Thus, when Brewer turned his attention to Pipeliner fins, he kept

Greg Noll Gun, 9'8"
In 1966, shaper Ben Aipa moved in for a long stint with the Greg Noll shop in Honolulu. He crafted this board in 1967 using double laminates and a 3/4-inch redwood stringer. Adopted 2001.

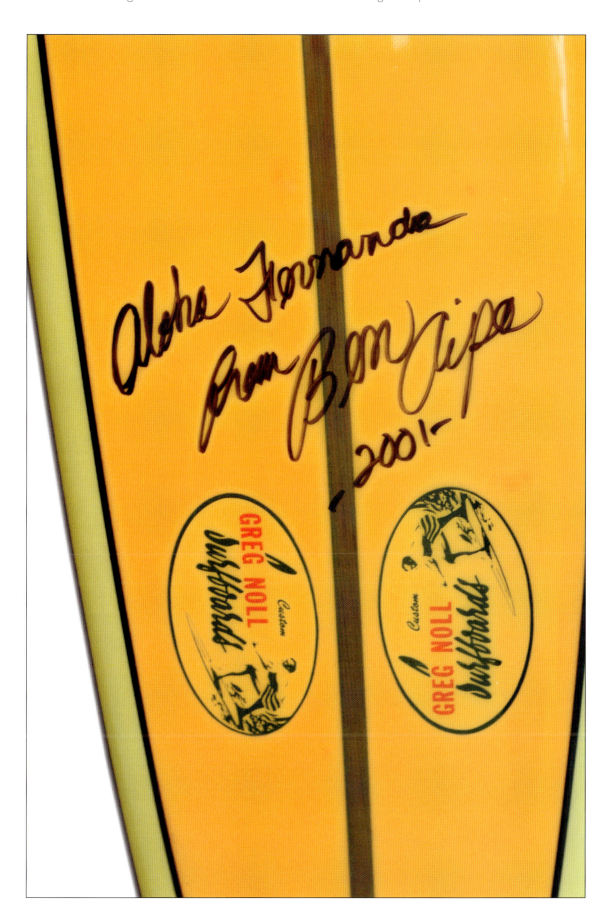

Greg Noll, 8'0"

This board features a transitional shape. It was most likely chopped off before being glassed to make a shorter board, right after the arrival of shortboards to the United States. Adopted 2004.

Greenough's concepts in mind. Working with Jimmy Lucas, Brewer reduced the area of the fins while keeping their 10 1/2-inch depth. Their "new moon" shape had a 5 1/2-inch base, which test riders Nuuhiwa and Jock Sutherland gave the thumbs up to back in California.

The Not-So-Little Mini-Gun

It was during summer 1967 that the roots of Brewer's shorter surfboards first began to sprout—and it was all an accident, according to Brewer and Randy Rarick, who were both working at Surfline Hawaii. As Drew Kampion wrote in *The Surfer's Journal*, "Dick Brewer claims to have made a short 'mini-gun' for Gary Chapman earlier in 1967—before Nat and crew dipped so much as a big toe into the futuristic waters of Honolua Bay. His recollection is clear: 'I'd made a 9-foot 10-inch gun for David Nuuhiwa in the spring of '67, and David broke the nose off, so I redrew it at 7 feet 8 inches with a 17-inch nose on it—a tanker nose—and Randy Rarick was a patcher and he reglassed it. I took that board out and rode it at Chun's, at the left called Piddlies—phenomenal roller coasters with that heavy nose and the gun tail. That board became the prototype for the Bing Lotus. So, the mini-gun was happening in the spring of '67.'"

Rarick's recollection was also clear: "I was a ding repairman working in town behind Surfline," Rarick told Kampion, "and Brewer was working there for Bing. Pintails were the rage, and in '67, he made one for David Nuuhiwa, and David broke

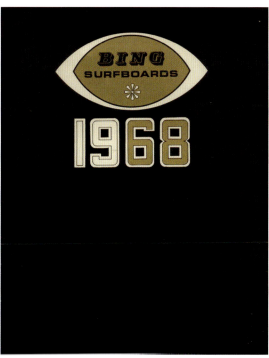

Bing Brochure, 1968

the nose off two feet back. So the board came in to me at Surfline repair, and I took the grinder and just rounded off the nose and patched it, and then Brewer comes in and looks at it, and he goes, 'Yeah, okay.' So Nuuhiwa took it back out and made it ride great . . . and that may have developed into the pocket rocket."

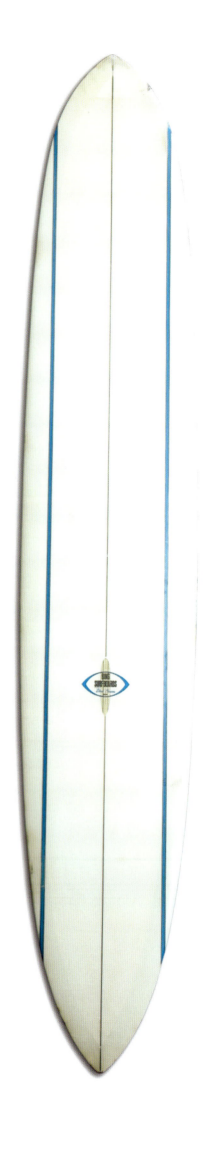

Bing Copeland Pipeliner, 10'3"

This board was made in 1968 in Hawai'i at the Surfline Hawaii shop. It was most likely shaped by Dick Brewer, although Gerry Lopez also shaped a few of these Pipeliners. Bing certified the board's history in a 1998 letter to the board's previous owner, Bob Kelly. Adopted 1998.

For some reason, all of this innovation led to Brewer being relieved of his command at Bing. Gary Chapman had purchased a reject blank and carried it over to Bing's factory where Brewer shaped it into an 8-foot 6-inch mini-gun. "Bing fired me the next day," Brewer told Kampion. "Before I left, I told all the shapers in California to shape underground, with the intent of wrecking the surfboard industry,

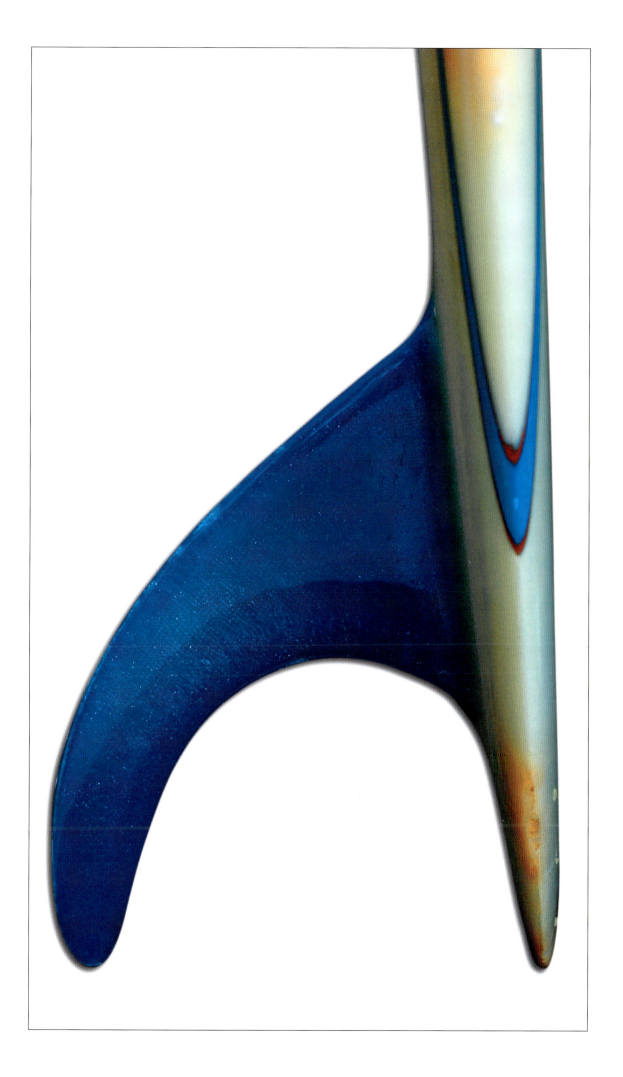

Reef Longboard, 9'2"
The history and origin of this mid-1960s board is unknown. Adopted 2001.

as it eventually did—at least as we knew it." But the story only began here. Barry Kanaiaupuni took that Chapman pocket rocket for a ride at Velzyland and pronounced it a winner. "Power off the bottom, roller coasters off the top . . . the board was brilliant, a door-opener," Brewer remembered.

Now Brewer went underground with his innovations. Setting up shop in Lahaina on Maui, he continued shaping and experimenting under the Lahaina Surf Designs (LSD) label. He was in the right place at the right time, as California-Hawai'i thinking on the future of high-performance surfboards was about to meet in a swift collision with the Australian school.

The 1967 Duke Kahanamoku contest invited the Australians, including Nat Young and Bob McTavish. The show was held in smaller surf at Sunset, and the change in performance was there for all to see. Rarick remembered the time for *The Surfer's Journal*: "It was a major transition year. The year Bob McTavish and Nat Young brought their V-bottoms to Hawai'i. I was pretty well connected in town. I was riding for Dewey Weber, working at the SurfLine shop patching boards, and Fred Van Dyke had asked me to work at the Duke Classic that year. So McTavish shows up, and we're talkin' wide tail, heavy V, big fin; some really dynamic changes when everybody else was riding pintails. They held the Duke on an 8- to 10-foot day at Sunset, and I remember standing next to Dewey as McTavish took off on this wave and just laid that thing over on the V panel. The thing slid about 3 feet. If he didn't have that huge fin, he would have

spun out, but he caught it, then angled up on like a 45-degree turn that nobody else was doing. It was such a different track. I remember I looked over at Dewey and went, 'Oh, my God.' And Dewey went, 'Something's happening here.' And that's when Dewey was king. He was selling more boards than anybody. I decided right then and there that I was gonna go to Australia. Those guys were onto something entirely new."

Jock Sutherland won the 1967 Duke, but another competition took place soon after. On the island of Maui in November, the Brewer guys on their mini-guns met with the McTavish mob on their deep, vee-bottomed haulers. As McTavish remembered to Ben Marcus for this book: "November was our big mistake. I made two boards for Hawaii. I left the 9-foot gun behind, and just took the overblown Plastic Machine. Although I was paid out as the 'spin-out king' at Sunset, to be fair I also got barrelled there, and climb-and-dropped all over Ricky Grigg's wake as he aimed for the shoulder with his arms held aloft as if he was conquering the joint! After Honolua, I never rode a Plastic Machine again till a few months ago. At least it opened the door."

While on Maui, there was some back and forth between McTavish and Brewer, and some of that back and forth was a saw's motion cutting the length of surfboards by inches and even feet. "RB [Brewer] had just shaped a board for Reno, 9-foot 6-inch pintail," McTavish said in *The Surfer's Journal*. "In the Maui shaping bay, I picked up a saw and placed it one foot from the tail, right on the finished blank. I looked Brewer in the eye; he looked me back. There was a pause. Then a faint smile crept over his

mouth, so I started cutting. I sawed a foot off it! He fared it out, and next week Reno won Makaha on it, they say! An 8-foot 6-inch squaretail. That was short for December 1967 in Maui. After hanging out with RB on Maui, I followed his lead into fluid lines, but not long needles as he was making. His *smallest* board in December was 9 feet 6 inches! Don't forget that! *That* was the mini-gun! Nine feet 6 inches! All Australia was on 7 feet 6 inches for hot dudes, to 8 feet 6 inches for retards."

Gerry Lopez supports that story with his own recollection: "I think it was in late '67," he told Drew Kampion. "Brewer had just moved over to Maui from the North Shore and was shaping in Lahaina. Reno [Abellira] and I each took a blank over there to get our boards made by him. Reno got his shaped first, but before he could shape mine, Nat and Greenough and McTavish and Ted Spencer and a couple of other Aussies showed up with those wide-tailed, vee-bottom boards. They wanted to go ride 'em at Honolua Bay, but there wasn't any surf there. John Thurston had a surf shop [at the Cannery in Lahaina] where all the boards were glassed, and they came there, and we met 'em, and Brewer and McTavish kind of bullshitted for a long time. So the next

day we go back to do my board—I think I wanted like a 9-foot 8-inch, which was considered a shorter board then—and Brewer just takes the saw and cuts a foot off the blank, and it's 8 feet 6 inches, and he tells me, 'That's how big a board you're getting."

During winter 1967–1968, Herbie Fletcher was part of a movement of guys on mini-guns, away from the traditional big-wave spot at Sunset Beach down to the hollower, shorter, barreling waves at Pipeline. "Back then everyone went down to surf Sunset," Fletcher said to Ben Marcus. "You don't see too many pictures of Pipeline in those days. Not until 1969 when Brewer showed up, no one came down to Pipeline and Backdoor. It was just our spot. And then after the World Contest, Gary Chapman and I moved into a house at Off the Wall before it was called Off the Wall. There were all these perfect rights coming down the beach at Pipeline because it would be small. Everyone in those days was big-wave riding so everyone hung out at Sunset, Haleiwa, Waimea. People didn't go to Pipeline. They thought it was too small or just a beachbreak. And so I grew up on beachbreaks and hotdogging. We moved in there and it was the first year of the mini-gun and Brewer was shaping at a house up at Bummer Hill, as

**Dewey Weber
"The Ski," 6'8"**
*Bearing a team logo
on the deck and a sun
logo on the bottom,
this 1969 Weber board
is fitted with a guid-
ance fin system.
Adopted 2001.*

Greg Noll "No Nose," 7'6"

This transitional board dates from 1969. It features a wide, round tail and a narrow, pulled-in, and flipped-up "no nose." It's also stringerless with a black pin-line on the lap and features the Fins Unlimited Vari-Set fin system. With a wild sticker, who knows where they were going with this shape? Adopted 2005.

we called it, and we were making boards and they were going shorter and then we moved into that house in January. . . . We called it Pipeline Rights, because there were rights coming down the beach, and then in 1968 people started calling it Off the Wall. I was surfing it with just a few guys: BK, Hakman, Chapman, Tiger Espere, Mike Hynson. Hynson moved in right next door to us, and he had a shaping room so he was making lots of boards and experimenting a lot. He was sort of the same size I am and same style and he had money and he would make all kinds of surfboards and experiment with them and I was right there getting all the advantages of it and I felt really privileged to be. . . . Hynson was the guru. The Maharishi, as he was called."

That winter began with mini-guns around 8 feet 6 inches, but as the winter progressed and the surfing got deeper, the boards got shorter. As Fletcher recalled, "Then they went down to 8 feet 2 inches and 7 feet 9 inches, and they kept on going down. For those days we surfed them just fine. We surfed it great. We were carving off the bottom, pulling in the tube on the nose and cutting back and really hotdogging the thing. Something the

older guys couldn't do. All the big-wave riders were in there for survival."

In 1968, Brewer posed for a photograph that would become famous and sum up the times. He sits before the camera like a grinning, in-shape Buddha, framed by his two leading disciples—Reno Abellira and Gerry Lopez, who are standing on their heads. The image perfectly captured Brewer as the world's leading rebel shaper, in direct opposition to the Australian shortboard revolution. As Drew Kampion wrote in *The Surfer's Journal*, "While the American 'surf industry' rocked back on its heels and scurried back to the drawing board after the short vee-bottom board swooned the surfing world, frantically retrenching and retooling to accommodate the sudden shifts in function, fashion, and philosophy, RB was almost solitary as an alternative (if not exactly a naysayer) to this Southern swell, assimilating it and translating it into his own evolving vision of the modern surfboard."

That same year, Brewer's acolyte Abellira was Hawai'i's juniors division champ, and gave everyone a look into the next decade when he rode his purple, 6-foot 10-inch, 7-pound round tail at the World Surfing Championships in Puerto

Hayden
Kneeboard, 5'6"

Hayden's late-1960s, semi-transparent kneeboard was inspired by George Greenough shapes. This board survives in original, unrestored condition. Adopted 2006.

Greg Noll, 9'0"
Ben Aipa likely shaped this late-1960s Hawaiian board. It features 50/50 rails, and a fast down-the-line transitional outline. This board is unrestored, and includes a rare, original removable fin that is probably worth as much as the board itself. Adopted 2004.

Rico. Abellira made it to a final that was about equally Old School versus New School, Australian against American. Hawaiian Fred Hemmings won with classic Hawaiian style and deserved the honor. Abellira finished sixth, but his surfing was exciting and thoroughly modern and a glimpse of the future: smaller surfers doing big things on smaller surfboards.

The shortboard revolution was in full glory, on both sides of the Pacific. In Australia, writer John Witzig penned for *Surfer Magazine* a screed called "We're Tops Now!" trumpeting Australian successes in design, performance, and competition—and putting California solidly in second. Backing this up, Witzig's brother Paul released the surf movie *Evolution* in 1969, showcasing seventeen-year-old sensation Wayne Lynch from Victoria. Lynch was the first surfer to bank off the crest of a wave, his tight turns and dramatic cutbacks signaling the divide between the eras of the long- and shortboard.

Continued on page 175

Greg Noll Decal

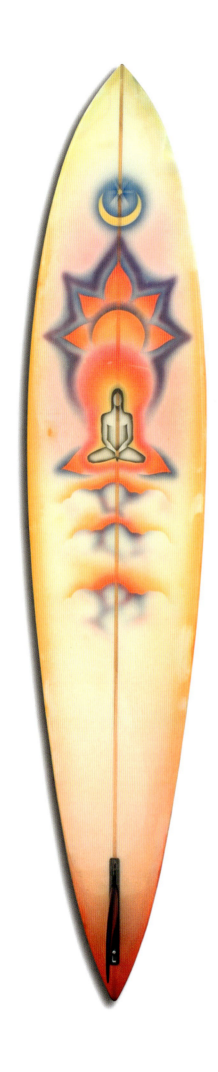
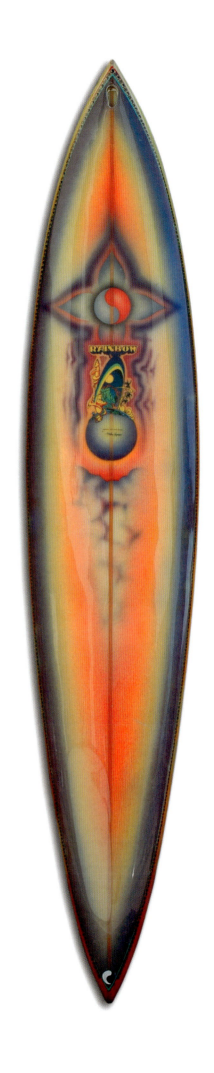

Mike Hynson Rainbow, 8'0"

A beautiful example of the psychedelic influence of the early 1970s by master shaper Mike Hynson. The exquisite airbrush and hand ink pin-line includes hundreds of hand-drawn "yin and yang" and "om" symbols in alternating order. This board has a weight plug on the nose and a single box fin. Adopted 2003.

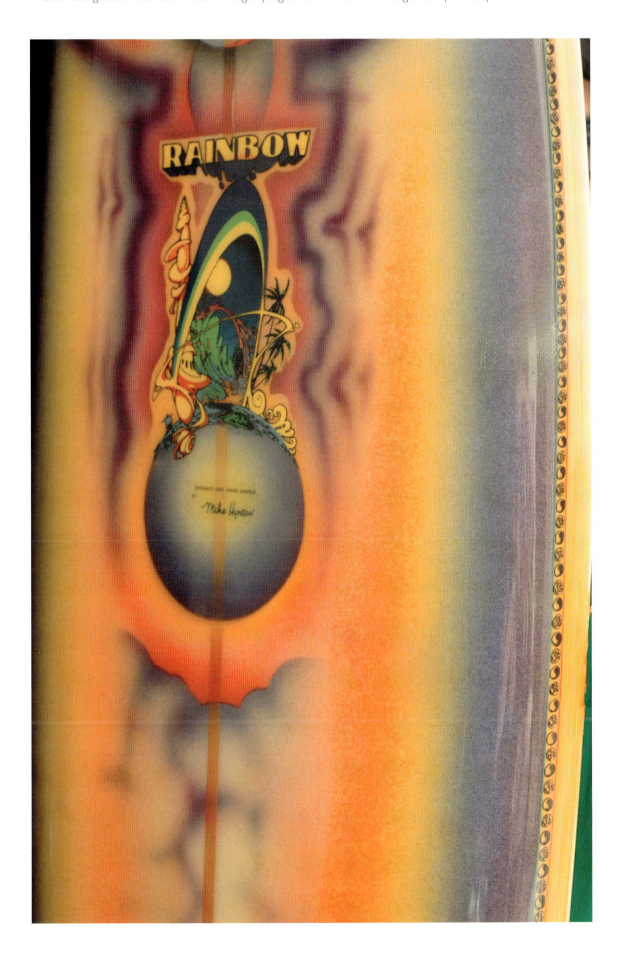

Mike Hynson, 1972
Out of the endless summer of the 1960s and into the purple haze of the 1970s, Hynson emerged as one of the best of the surfers and shapers. He rode a traditional longboard when he traveled the world with Robert August in 1964 to make The Endless Summer. Within ten years, Hynson was into very different things, and his experiments with foam, plastic, and other material earned him the nickname The Maharishi. Photograph © Jeff Divine

Surfboards Hawaii Ad, 1970

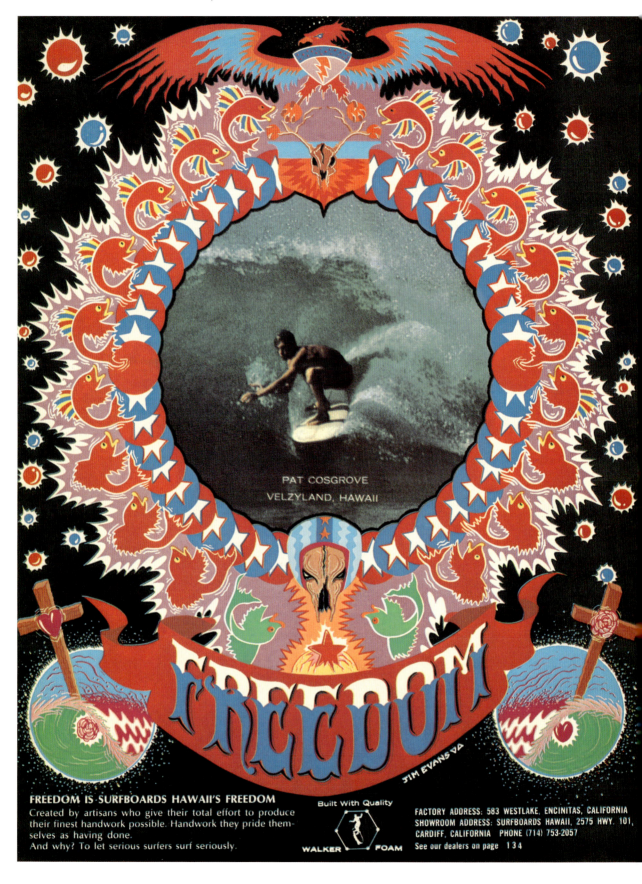

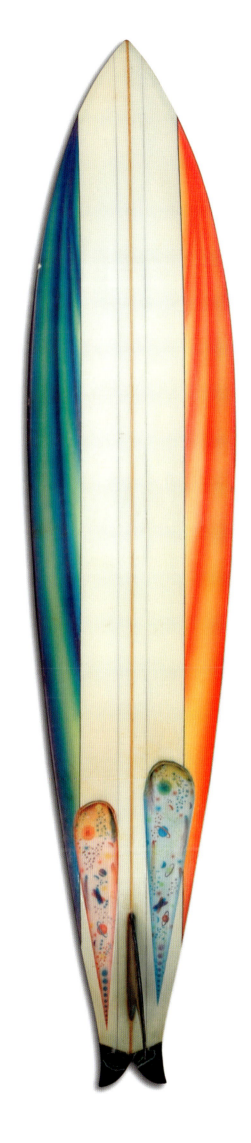

Vinny Bryan Futuristic, 7'6"
A typically trippy early 1970s board with psyche-delic airbrush artwork. The board features an air induction deck with exhaust channels in the bottom, a hollow dolphin fin, and a reverse chamber fishtail. Adopted 2001.

Continued from page 169
Gone Fishing

On December 4, 1969, Greg Noll was the last man standing on the biggest day of surf Oahu had ever seen. With the North Shore completely closed out, Noll and friends drove around to the West Side and replayed the ending of *Ride the Wild Surf.* Noll was the last man out the back on a truly massive day. He managed to catch a wave, wiped out at the bottom, made it to the beach, and then, like a modern Sisyphus, he packed it all up, moved to northern California, and went fishing.

Noll wasn't alone. Dewey Weber had been the leading surfboard manufacturer through the 1960s, and when the industry now went shorter and underground, he figured it was something short term that he could ride out. But the margins in the surf-board business were tight, and as for all the other mass-production surfboard makers of the day, the ride was over. Weber down-sized as fast as he could, but the financial toll was too heavy. In the early 1970s, he constructed a two-man swordfishing boat and he too was gone fishing.

The 1970s arrived amid a purple haze. Surfboards were being over-innovated in an era of drugged-out weirdness. Purple prose in the ads and brochures promised the heavens, but most of the boards failed to deliver the real thing. Steve Barilotti described the offerings in *The Surfer's Journal*: "Super-short, hyper-kicked noses boasted a brief moment in the sun. High-tech plastic honeycomb-cell was touted as the new god. WAVE of Ventura made hollow pop-out

Continued on page 179

Ocean Pacific Surfboards, 6'4"

A typical board shape and typical airbrushed artwork from the late 1970s. On loan.

Hobie Ad, 1970s

Hobie Ad, 1970s

In the Spirit of Hawaii

David Nuuhiwa/ David Nuuhiwa Surfboards

Duke Pahoa Kahanamoku, full-blooded Hawaiian, began surfing when he was eight-years-old, and became a legend before he was 25. Three-time Olympic Gold Medalist in swimming, incredible paddler and outrigger canoeist, the greatest surfer of all time, he brought the "spirit of aloha" to the world beyond Hawaii.

Duke Kahanamoku Surfwear introduces:

Trunks
Designed and sewn of only the highest quality materials, to hold up for seasons of rough Hawaiian water wear.

Walkshorts
Comfortable for living the mellow Hawaiian life style.

Shirts
Carefully matched and sewn from authentic Hawaiian prints, reflecting the colors and moods of the Islands.

All made and styled in Hawaii to serve the needs of active watermen around the world.

Duke Kahanamoku Made in Hawaii by *Catalina*

Duke Kahanamoku Ad, 1970s
David Nuuhiwa stands tall with a winged, swallowtail, twin-finned Fish.

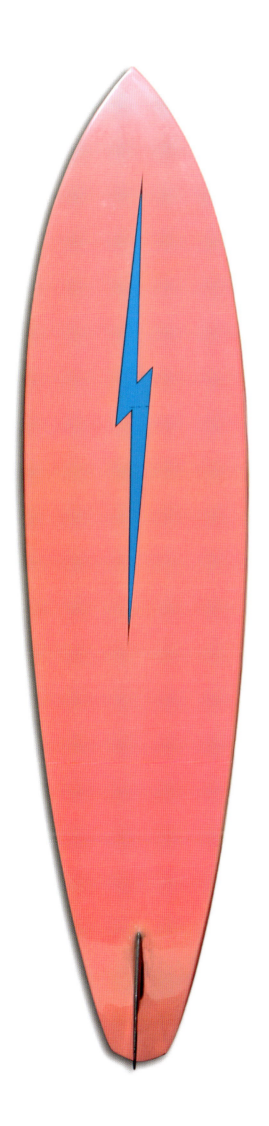

Gerry Lopez Lighting Bolt, 6'4"

This is a typical Lopez small-wave model, dating from 1974. It was shaped by Gerry and glassed by Jack Reeves. Adopted 2001.

Continued from page 174

boards with hollow fins. Hansen boards had "Super Vibes" while Corky Carroll offered "Space Sticks." The ultimate wacky 1970s board, however, was the Hendricks Omni with its handgrips, centerboard, rudder, and, of course, a speedometer. Leave it to Greg Noll to take them all to task. In a *Surfer Magazine* manifesto entitled "The B.S.'ers," he laid out the blame: 'The major offences committed in the name of the almighty dollar are too numerous to mention . . . but the best are the BS ads which have finally gotten to the point that nobody can begin to believe what they're trying to say, including the manufacturer who's running the ad.'"

Barilotti continued in *The Surfer's Journal*: "The shortboard revolution—sparked just three years earlier on the beaches of New South Wales with the 9-foot McTavish V-Bottom—was in tatters. The backlash proved profound. In 1970, Californian Rolf Aurness was the new world champ, returning the insult of the 1966 World Contest by beating the Australians at their homebreak in Johanna, Victoria. Aurness rode a pragmatic, streamlined 6-foot 10-inch pintail to take out the woefully under-gunned Australians, who had taken the shorter-is-better mantra to absurd lengths. Aurness stood out as the fastest and most precise surfer at the contest. Even Nat Young gave him kudos: 'Rolf was going twice as fast as we were and covering twice the ground.'"

Afterward, competitive surfing was deemed irrelevant if not downright harmful to one's newly discovered karma. California surfing retreated into acid-inspired black-wetsuit fundamentalism that

Shaun Tomson, 1970s *From the 1970s and into the 1980s, aristocratic South African Shaun Tomson lead a band of Merry Men from Australia and South Africa into a modern assault on the waves of the North Shore. Shaun rode Pipeline backside like no one had ridden it before, and he set a stage for the twenty-first-century deal where surfers with their left-foot forward now win most every Pipe Masters. Good surfboards were crucial to this new attack and this kind of surfing lead to the transition from the single-fin to the Thruster.* Photograph © Jeff Divine

Lightning Bolt Ad, 1970s
Team Bolt, lean and mean. From left: Jeff Hakman, Rory Russel, Gerry Lopez, and Reno Abellira.

**Gerry Lopez "Big Wednesday"
Lighting Bolt, 7'6"**
Custom-made and specially shaped for Fernando Aguerre by Gerry Lopez, with Gerry's inscription in Spanish. Adopted 2001.

rejected anything not 100 percent "natural." Surfing in the 1970s sung a mantra of turn off, tune out, and drop out.

Different Strokes, Different Folks

In 1970, Hawaiian surfer Ben Aipa decided to establish his own surfboard label. Aipa had been shaping since 1966, crafting the board Fred Hemmings used to win the 1968 world championship. His double-point swallowtails and split-rail stingers were being ridden by a great group of Hawaiian hotdoggers, including Larry Bertlemann, Michael Ho, Montgomery "Buttons" Kaluhiokalani, and Mark Liddel, who took Involvement surfing to a whole new level on both shores of Oahu and around the globe. Their surfing would inspire not just surfers, but skateboarders the world over. The roots of the Dogtown and Z Boyz skateboard revolution go straight back to those young Hawaiians all riding Aipa innovations and lighting up the 1970s behind Larry Bertlemann's battle cry: "Anything is possible!"

As most of the surfing world was going smaller and sleeker, Herbie Fletcher instead jumped onto the nose of a longboard in 1975, declaring in his ads, "The Thrill is Back!" "I had been in the mountains and out of the scene for a little bit," Fletcher admitted to Ben Marcus. "When I came back everyone was on shortboards. A lot of guys had quit surfing because they would go away to college or they would work and they didn't have time except maybe on the weekends or vacation time. They quit surfing because they couldn't

Continued on page 190

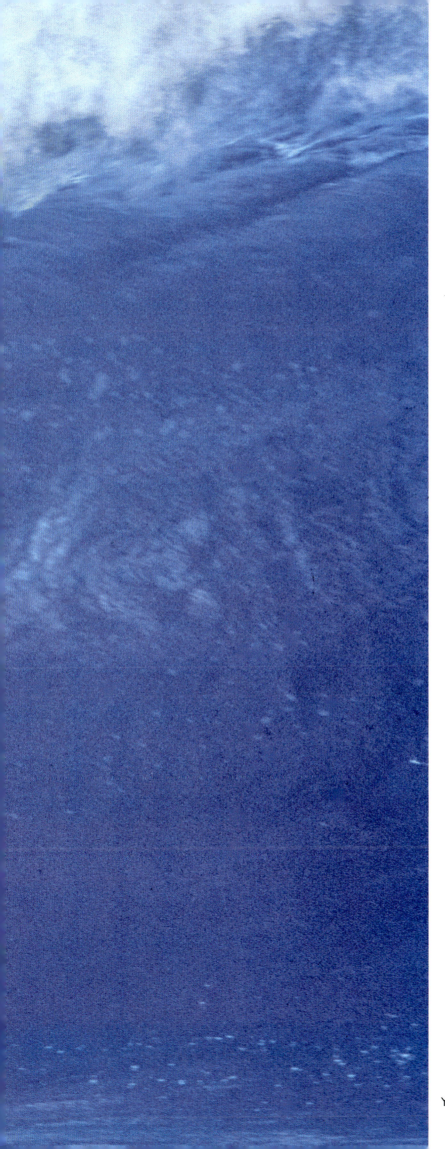

Gerry Lopez, 1970s

Throughout the 1970s, goofyfoot Lopez' precision surfing at Pipeline inspired a generation of surfers with his casual but daring approach to the world's most challenging wave. Lopez did it all on boards he made himself and branded with the Lightning Bolt. Following his lead, all the great surfers who came to Hawai'i rode Bolts as a sign of distinction, and the brand dominated maga-zines and movies into the 1980s. Photograph © Jeff Divine

Mark Richards Twin Fin, 6'0"

Mark hand-shaped this mid-1970s-style board for Fernando Aguerre. The board was part of a limited-edition reproduction of the original twin fins Mark rode during his four-world-championship run; this board is number 18. Adopted 2002.

Mark Richards, 1970s

By the standards of modern, twenty-first-century surfers, Mark Richards might as well have been Shaq: Big and gangly, with an awkward, knock-kneed style that somehow looked graceful and thrilled a generation. Richards needed no help in big Hawaiian or Australian surf, but his size put him at a disadvantage in the small stuff. Richards' experimentation with twin fins gave him a secret weapon that lead to four world titles, and the twin fin lead to the modern Thruster. Photograph © Jeff Divine

Spider Murphy, 7'2"

Hand-shaped by Spider Murphy for Fernando Aguerre, this board is number 001 of a limited-edition run. It is identical to the one ridden by Shaun Tomson during the Freeride/Off The Wall *sessions. Adopted 2002.*

Continued from page 183

ride the shortboard. So I go: Let's revert this back to the old beginning again, where it was fun. I started telling the world, 'The Thrill is Back!' and started making longboards for people who had families, who quit surfing. A lot of these guys had kids who were coming of an age and they wanted to go surfing with their kids. I sold a bunch of boards. Everybody was calling me from all over. Lots of in-land people, but the funny thing was Florida wasn't into it. They wanted to ride those short, shitty boards. They sat up in the water to their arm pits and watched me do circles around them. I would try to get them to get involved, but they were influenced by the magazines so they were on shortboards. Those guys who were buying the shortboards didn't know anything that wasn't printed in the magazines in the last six months to a year. They would look at the magazine and say, 'This is what is going on.'"

The Lightning Bolt Strikes

Into the mid 1970s, goofyfoot surfer Gerry Lopez was becoming the universally acknowledged master of Pipeline, but he had also been shaping on the side since 1968. He and surfing judge Jack Shipley were both working at a Honolulu surf shop called Surf Line Hawaii, but now in 1970 they bought the old Hobie outlet on Kapiolani Boulevard. Lopez had been fixing a colored lightning bolt emblem to his boards since 1969, and so they now named their shop Lightning Bolt Surfboards.

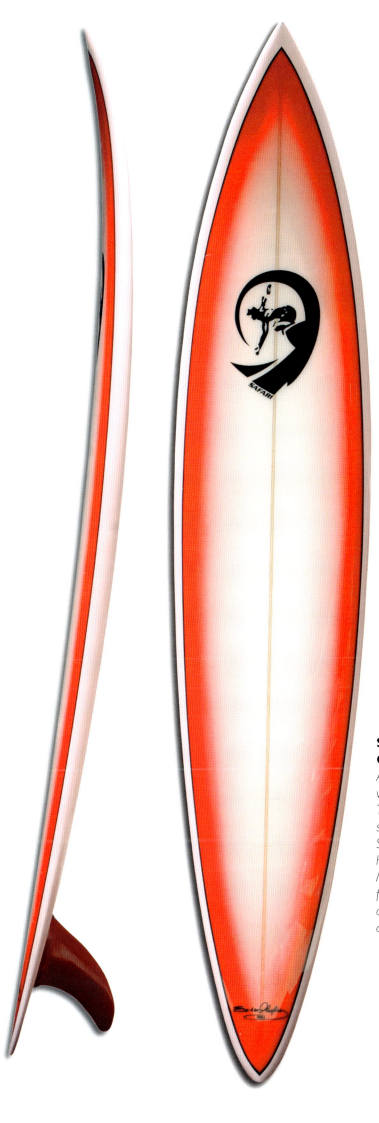

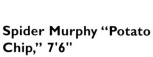

Spider Murphy "Potato Chip," 7'6"

A replica of Shaun Tomson's secret weapon "Potato Chip" from 1975. The original was a hyper-kicked, super-thin, super-wide board that Shaun kept out of public view until he paddled out. He won the Pipe Masters on the original board—the first regularfoot to win the event— and paved the way for Kelly Slater and much to come. Adopted 2004.

Surfboard Shaping Company Stinger Swallow, 7'3"

This 1977 Stinger Swallow was shaped by Harold "Iggy" Ige after leaving Dewey Weber and moving back to Hawai'i. Iggy's boards were surfed by Bobby Owens and Lynne Boyer. Adopted 2003.

Both Lopez and Reno Abellira learned their craft at the feet of Dick Brewer, and now Abellira was one of the first hires at Lightning Bolt as he was a great surfer and fine shaper. As early as 1970–1971, Brewer and Abellira had experimented on a tri-fin surfboard, but that design was ahead of its time and there would be many trials and errors over the next decade before the three-finned board became the standard.

By the mid-1970s, Lightning Bolt had become an elite boutique. Hawaiian shapers Bill Barnfield, Tom Parrish, Reno Abellira, Barry Kanaiaupuni, Tom Nellis, and Tom Eberly were all crafting boards out of their houses and bringing them to the Bolt retail store, all of them trimmed with that electric logo that dominated magazines and movies in a way that few labels ever have. Part of this was due to clever marketing, as Shipley generously handed out beautiful Bolt guns to all the top surfers who came to the North Shore. Thus, a lot of Lightning Bolt logos appeared magically on magazine covers and in surf movies.

Two of the top shapers for Bolt during this time were Tom Parrish and Bill Barnfield. Born in Southern California, Parrish began surfing at twelve and began making boards at seventeen. He moved to Hawai'i in 1969 and worked for Surf Line Hawaii and Country Surfboards before taking up with Lightning Bolt in 1972. His big-wave guns were renowned for their elegance, with gracefully rounded pintails—so much so that *Surfing Magazine* hailed Parrish as "the man with the red-hot planer."

Barnfield was also California-born, shaping his first board at age 20. Into the early 1970s, he founded Evergreen Surfboards in Oregon, and helped Al Merrick get his Channel Islands Surfboards going in Santa Barbara. He signed on with Lightning

Bill Caster Single Fin, 7'10"

A great 1980 example of the legendary late La Jolla shaper Bill Caster's work. This single fin is in fine, unrestored condition. Adopted 2006.

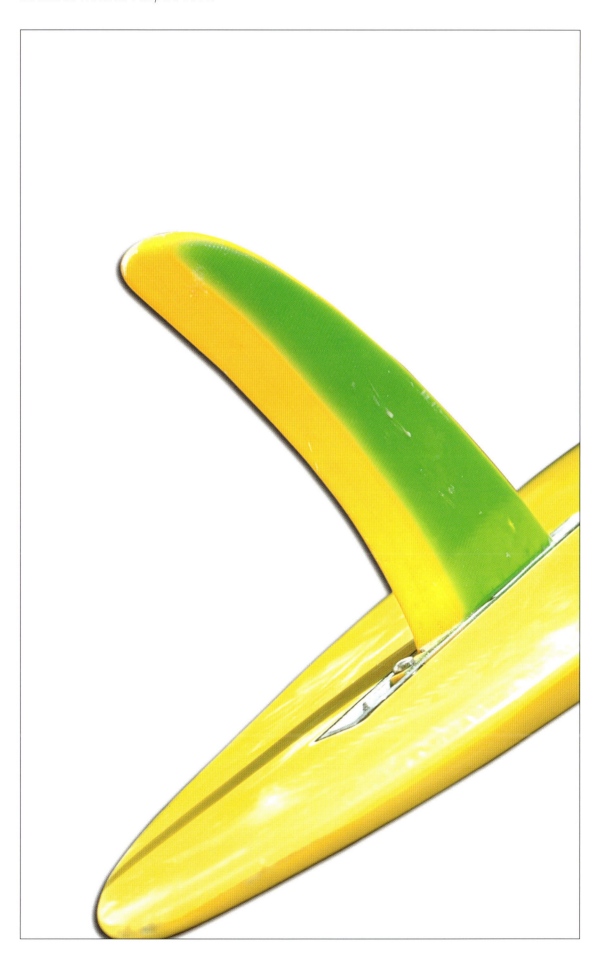

Infinity Surfboards, 6'0"
This 1980 board features custom bikini artwork.
Adopted 2006.

Bolt in 1973, and was one of the men behind the planer as Hawaiian surfboards became thinner, narrower, and more refined.

From 1973 to 1978, the vast majority of the best surfers in Hawai'i were riding Lightning Bolts, from Mark Richards to Margo Oberg, Jeff Hakman to Rory Russell. Yet of all the surfers who rode Lightning Bolts, owner Gerry Lopez was arguably the most famous. In 1972, he starred in Greg MacGillivray's *Five Summer Stories*, which featured Lopez in super-slow motion proving his credo that "Pipeline is a cakewalk if you know how." Studying Lopez' catlike approach to Pipeline, the finer traits of Lightning Bolts were there to be appreciated by one and all, and Lopez almost single-handedly imprinted the Bolt brand on the minds of surfers around the globe.

The Multi-Fins

At the dawn of the 1970s, the two Campbell brothers from Ventura, California, were working on a far-out, three-finned board with channels they called the "Bonzer." They borrowed the name of the board from the Australians—it meant "good," or better yet, "bitchin'"—and the design was truly that. They built their first board in November 1970, using a 5-foot 4-inch kneeboard shaped from a Clark Foam reject blank. The middle fin was big and boxy and placed well back on a squashtail, while the side fins were long, plastic blades put well forward of the center fin. The board was different—and must have been a bastard to shape and glass.

At the 1972 World Championship back in Ocean Beach, Hawaiian surfer Jim Blears and Nuuhiwa finished first and

second, respectively, both of them riding the novel Steve Lis-designed Fish. Lis was a kneeboarder, and he crafted the Fish in 1967, later transferring the design into a standup board. The blunt-nosed, twin-fin surfboard had a low rocker and a split-tail.

The twin-fin design harked back to the "dual-fin" surfboards Bob Simmons made in the 1940s and 1950s. Simmons was riding a dual-fin board in 1954 when he drowned at Windansea, and the design was revived in 1967 by Barry "Bear" Mirandon as the Twin-Pin Model while working for La Jolla Surfboards. This early twin-fin fascination came and went quickly.

The Campbells saw twin-fins come and go, but they thought their Bonzer had more to offer. In early 1973, they took it to the power centers of the surf industrial complex. Dewey Weber was still going, but after initial enthusiasm he showed the brothers the door. Down the street in Hermosa Beach, they talked to Bing Copeland and his head shaper Mike Eaton, who liked the Campbells' technical explanation.

The Campbells and Bing signed a deal paying two dollars a board. Bing saw it as a way to make a connection to the garage shapers that were threatening the established labels: "It became the in thing to have a no-name or garage-built board for the 'in group,'" Copeland told Barilotti. "This made it difficult for the major manufacturers to compete, due to the fact that the backyard builders could buy blanks and all the materials needed at basically the same cost as we paid, and they had no overhead."

Eaton introduced the Bonzer to the North Shore in May 1973. Eaton liked how they soaked up the power at Sunset, and when he talked Jeff Hakman into riding

The Thruster from Down Under

Take the twin fins of Mark Richards, Reno Abellira, and others; mix in the three-finned, channel-bottomed Bonzers fashioned by the Campbell Brothers; throw in a little Dick Brewer, Ben Aipa, and more; and you have the three-finned Thruster. This board revolutionized every-thing in 1981, as the three fins provided the high speed, holding power, and directional stability that modern surfers craved. Photograph © Jeff Divine

one, Hakman was sold too. Bing hyped the Bonzer hard with magazine ads, and the board lived up to the hype when Ian Cairns rode one to victory at the 1973 Smirnoff Contest at Laniakea, defeating Hakman. The design went down to Australia where it was scoffed at as a Seppo gimmick, until Peter Townend beat Michael Peterson and Bruce Raymond on a Bonzer at the Newcastle Open Surf Titles in 1974.

And then, for a variety of reasons, the Bonzer fizzled. There were production problems with a board that was hard to shape and hard to glass and hard to sand. Bing sold out to G&S Surfboards in 1974, and the production problems increased: "There was no relationship with Larry Gordon or any real care of Bonzer quality control," Duncan Campbell told Barilotti. "To G&S, Bonzers were just another line of boards that were being offered. They had no real understanding of how they worked."

The Campbells parted company with G&S in 1975, even refusing royalties from the shoddily made Bonzers. So it all didn't end well, but only a few years later, an Australian surfer named Simon Anderson would prove the Campbells right. "We championed the three-fin cause for ten years before the world caught on with Simon's Thruster," Duncan Campbell told Barilotti. "But it came true. Nobody can say that three-fins didn't become the best high-performance surfboards. You can't do as much on a single-fin. Kelly Slater at his peak surfing ability couldn't have won the world championship on a single-fin surfboard. Someone on a Thruster would have beat him."

Twin-Fin Developments

Tom Morey's Noseriding Invitational of 1965 was the first surf contest to offer a prize purse. Over the next few years, there were a growing number of professional surf contests in Hawai'i, California, Australia, and Peru. Pro surfing had caught on and through the rest of the 1970s, the prize money grew and the surfing world began to take it all seriously. Those incentives of money and fame helped to spur on the development and design of surfboards.

Reno Abellira had experimented with an early version of the tri-fin with Dick Brewer in the early 1970s, and in 1977, it was one of Abellira's stubby, double-keeled Fish that inspired Mark Richards to shape twin-fins. Richards was a tall, gangly bloke with a funny grin who had been shaping his own surfboards since he was fifteen. As a surfer, he had an unusual, knock-kneed style that was goofy in small waves but brilliant in perfect waves at Honolua Bay and Sunset. But because of his size, he was at a disadvantage in smaller surf against smaller guys. Now, in 1976, when Abellira came to Australia with a wide, blunt-nosed 5-foot 3-incher with two fins, Richards took notes. The following year, he did a one-month apprenticeship with Dick Brewer and was soon producing a longer, more-streamlined version of the twin-fin.

South African Shaun Tomson won the world title in 1977, followed by Wayne "Rabbit" Bartholomew in 1978. But in 1979, Richards won the first of his four world titles, in part because the twin-fin became his secret weapon in smaller surf.

Enter the Thruster

If Simon Anderson's father hadn't won the lottery, where would surfing be today? Anderson was born in 1954 and was living in the inland Australian suburb of Balgowlah when his dad got lucky

Simon Anderson, 1981

A big bloke, Simon searched for a secret weapon to give him the power and performance he needed in small and large waves. Single-fins weren't cutting it and twin-fins weren't enough, so Simon put one and two together and came up with the Thruster. Anderson won the Pipe Masters on a Thruster in 1981, and the board has been the standard ever since. If only he had patented that design. . . .
Photograph © Jeff Divine

Welcome to the Machine

In the late 1970s, French surfer-shaper-engineer Michel Barland developed the first commercial computerized shaping machine. Barland began surfing in France in 1957 and built his first surfboard that year from plywood. In 1962, Barland won the French Surfing Championships, and by 1968, he graduated from the University of Paris with a degree in mechanical engineering. That same year, Barland became the European licensee for Clark Foam, and over the years, Clark regularly incorporated Barland's design and equipment advances. In 1979, Barland applied his surfing and shaping knowledge with his mechanical engineering degree to design his computerized shaping machine. By the early 1980s, Barland could key in fifty variables, hit a button, and thirteen minutes later have a mechanically shaped surfboard blank that required just a few minutes of additional fine sanding. Fifteen years later, most major board manufacturers around the world would be using an updated version of Barland's shaping machine.

on the lottery and moved the family to a beachfront house at Collaroy, near Narrabeen. Simon got his first surfboard in 1967 at thirteen. By 1971, he was a towering, 6-foot 3-inch seventeen-year-old red-hot surfer, winning the juniors division at the Australian National Titles and the Bells Beach contest. He defended both titles successfully in 1972 and made the Australian team for the World Surfing Championships. Anderson was a big bloke who was still filling into himself then, but he had a smooth, powerful, easygoing style that even his foes loved to watch.

By October 1980, Anderson, like every other pro surfer, was looking for a secret weapon akin to Mark Richard's twin-fin. Pro surfing was getting big, and even a big bloke could make a decent living from it and have a good time surfing around the world—if he had the talent and the equipment.

Anderson's problem was similar to Richards': He was a big guy who had it easy in the big stuff, yet suffered in small surf. So, Anderson tried to shape his own

twin-fin, but he couldn't get it right. Then, in 1980, he began making a version of Geoff McCoy's "no-nose" board, with a wide nose and narrower tail and with extra vee and a rail pivot wing. This gave him more vertical, snappy turns, but it still wasn't the secret weapon he envisioned.

Still searching, in late 1980 Anderson ran across shaper Frank Williams and his twin-fin fitted with an extra, small keel in the center. Anderson returned to his skunkworks and added three fins to his no-nose design. Anderson surfed his new creation, liked it, and christened it with the name "Thruster" for the thrust the extra fin added to his turning.

He carried the Thruster to Hawai'i and then California in winter 1980, letting his friends test it. He also showed it to board makers like Rusty Preisendorfer and Gary McNabb, and finally McNabb and Nectar Surfboards in California decided to build versions.

Historian Nick Carroll emailed his remembrances of Anderson and the Thruster, circa 1981: "Back in Oz, early

1981, several other shapers, including Phil Byrne, made some three-fins off Simon's measurements. Others laughed it off. At the first competitive test for the Thruster—the Stubbies event in Queensland, Simon got a 17th. Some other Aussies surfed their own versions, including Tom Carroll on a Byrne, but Carroll reverted to a twinnie in the small conditions. Shaun Tomson free-surfed it at Burleigh and asked Simon to make one. After the Stubbies event, Simon then went to Bells and blew everyone away with his performance level in large and small surf. He won by beating Cheyne in 3-foot waves, but it was really the 15-foot day that convinced everyone the board could work. Others to surf The Board that day included Marc Price and Wayne Lynch. Three weeks later Simon won the Surfabout in excellent 5-foot Narrabeen, in epic heats against Dane Kealoha and Shaun Tomson. Anderson didn't compete in about a third of the events that year, and finished sixth in the world as Mark

Richards won the world title again. Yet Anderson finally had his secret weapon and proved himself the breakthrough surfer of the year."

By mid-1981, most every pro surfer was riding a Thruster—thanks in large part to Anderson's generosity and willingness to share his board measurements with all. Taking ideas going back to Bob Simmons' "dual-fin" design of the 1940s and 1950s through the Lis Fish, the Bonzer, and the twin-fins of Dick Brewer, Reno Abellira, Mark Richards, and others, Anderson's Thruster has been the design of choice ever since. "It took a long time and a lot of designing to really bring out the best in the Thruster idea," Nick Carroll wrote. "Basically the thruster stuck a V-8 in the Kombi wagon that was the single-fin surfboard of 1980." Amazingly, Anderson chose not to patent his design, and the world's shapers and makers were free to copy it. As Nick Carroll noted, "Simon is not rich, but he makes Kelly's pointbreak boards, and Kelly's rich as creosote."

CHAPTER 8

Brave New World

The More Things Change, the More They Stay the Same

1981 AND STILL GOING STRONG

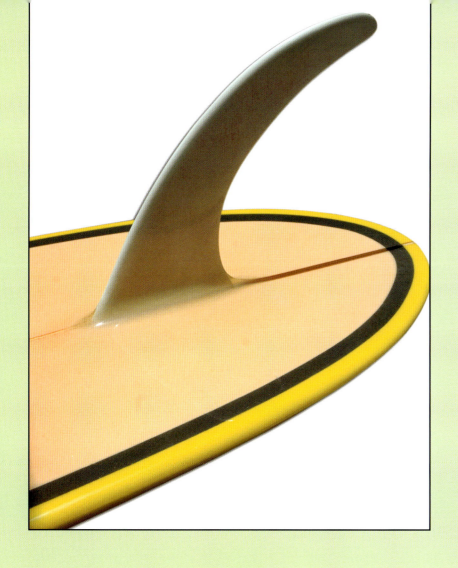

D ave Parmenter is in many ways the modern incarnation of Tom Blake, with a little bit of Bob Simmons, Pat Curren, and George Greenough thrown in for good measure. A modern-day coast *haole* who fell equally in love with surfing and the surfboard, Parmenter was a professional surfer in the 1980s who now splits his time between California's Central Coast and Oahu's West Side. He shapes custom boards for friends and clients, and keeps an eye on the modern world from an overview of experience and brains. Bright, opinionated, eloquent, knowledgeable, and unafraid, for the past twenty years Parmenter has written occasional manifestos on style, courage, trends, and surfboard fashions, his word generally considered the Burning Bush in a world where experience and eloquence don't often come together in one and the same person.

In the early 1990s, Parmenter penned a manifesto, "Thoroughly Modern Silly," for *Surfer Magazine* in which he questioned the trend toward extremely light, thin, narrow shortboards. He wrote, "For the first time in surfing history, the boards being ridden by the pros or 'the elite' cannot be ridden

**Wayne Lynch
Evolution, 8'0"**

Opposite Page:
**Simon Anderson
Energy Thruster,
5'10"**
*This historic tri-fin Thruster
was shaped by Anderson
on the North Shore in
1981, shortly after his Pipe
Masters win.*

by the average surfer. From Phil Edwards to Tom Curren, the best surfer in the world rode boards that the typical surfer should have had under his feet as well. But the past decade of pro surfing has, thanks to the Slop Factor, pared down the average size and weight of the top surfers with a ruthless evolutionary purge. Once, Thunderlizards like Simon Anderson and Ian Cairns strode through the pageantry, and average weights were up around 170 pounds. Today, with a climactic shift from Sunset to Sao Paulo, the scene is fraught with compact little Saurian roosters, 125 to 130 pounds, riding short, ultra-thin, hyper-rockered miniaturized surfboards."

Parmenter referred to a trend in which the best surfers in the world had shrunk from the big blokes who pioneered pro surfing, twin fins, deeper tube-riding, and Thrusters—Mark Richards, Shaun Tomson, Ian Cairns, Simon Anderson—to a new era where pro surfers were specialized to the size of gymnasts. The pro surfers of the early 1990s were uniformly small, light, strong, and very fast, and the surfboards designed for them were almost impossibly thin and narrow. And almost impossible for the average surfer to ride.

The Thrust of the Thruster

Australian surfer and board designer Simon Anderson proved that it's possible to be too good of a bloke. In 1980, Anderson crafted his Thruster surfboard, a square-tailer fitted with three, small like-sized fins designed to boost the thrust in the board's turns. He promptly scored several contest wins atop his tri-fin, and then won the 1981 Surfabout championship. Yet Anderson

Simon Anderson Energy Thruster, 5'10"
Becky Benson went on to the win the OP Pro riding this board in 1981 as well. Adopted 2001.

Peter Schroff, 5'9"

This early 1980s shortie hotdogger's board features a quadruple fin setup. On loan.

Sean Bradbury "Hydrofoils," 6'2"

Custom-shaped for Fernando Aguerre, this board bears the first-generation original "Reef Brazil" rice paper logos and first-generation noseguard and Trac-Top traction system with "Secret Weapon" arch bar. Adopted 1986.

Dave Rastovich, 2000s

Modern surfing is all about speed, and Dave Rastovich is one of the fastest surfers of the early twenty-first century. Speed down the face, speed off the bottom, speed back up the face, and enough speed to break the bonds of gravity and go orbital for a few moments. This is Rastovich at an Indian Ocean launching pad. Photograph © Jeff Divine

Skip Frye Swallowtail, Simmons influenced, 7'4"

Influenced by a Bob Simmons design, this board was custom-shaped and signed by master shaper and glide specialist Skip Frye for "Fernando of the Reef" for a trip to Costa Rica in 1994. It was hand-painted by Argentinean artist Soledad de la Riva in 2000.

neglected to patent his tri-fin design, and it became a gift to the surfing world.

The Thruster was adopted and then advanced by shapers around the surfing world. Al Merrick of Santa Barbara added much of the fine-tuning to the tri-fin design; as he admitted in 1987: "I'm a designer but I haven't discovered anything," Merrick was quoted in Matt Warshaw's *The Encyclopedia of Surfing*. "I'm just using what's been around before . . . and I'm sure I'll take more ideas from somebody in the future." By the mid-1980s, the Thruster was the board of choice for most every surfer around the globe.

In 1986, Tom Curren won the first of three world titles riding a Channel Islands Thruster shaped by Merrick, winning again in 1987 and 1990. Curren's style set professional surfing on a path it's still following in the 2000s, but his stance went straight back to the mode established by Miki Dora in the 1960s: Keep the arms low, the upper body quiet, and let the board do all the moving and talking. Curren's surfing was incredibly smooth, fast, and deep, and his preternatural wave judgment and ocean knowledge inspired writer Derek Hynd to stand up in front of everyone at a Steamer Lane surf contest in the 1990s and proclaim, "Tom Curren is the ocean!"

The cutting-edge Thruster shortboard became more refined under the hands of shapers like Merrick and Rusty Preisendorfer in California as well as Hawaiians includ-

Gary Linden Agave Gun, 9'6"
*Gary personally harvested the agave pieces
and glued them together to generate this rare
and beautiful blank. Shaped and signed by
Gary. Adopted 2000.*

**Gary Linden
Balsa Gun, 9'0"**
*This lightweight
big-wave gun was
shaped by Gary
in 1999.*

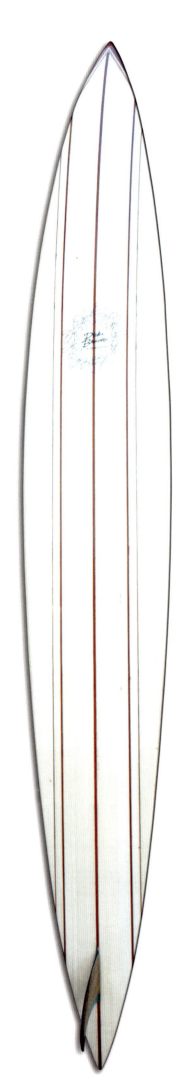

Dick Brewer Balsa Gun, 12'0"
This mammoth Rhino Chaser balsa gun from 2000 boasts redwood stringers. It was hand-shaped and signed by Brewer, and brought from Hawai'i by Randy Rarick. Adopted 2000.

ing John Carper and Pat Rawson. And it continued to win under the feet of Curren and world champions Damien Hardman and Derek Ho. Still, there were other surfboard design ideas afloat.

Something Old, Something New

The longboard revolution begun by Herbie Fletcher in 1975 was slowly being accepted by a surfing world who equated riding longboards with pushing yourself around in a wheelchair. Going into the 1990s, credible surfers like Joel Tudor in San Diego and Jay Moriarity in Santa Cruz boldly let the world know that it was okay to start on a longboard and stay on a longboard. Throughout the decade, there was a level-headed trend to ride the board that conditions demanded and not just stay on your shortboard and sink.

In 1985, Santa Barbara's John Bradbury began futzing around with epoxy, a resin that was stronger and more durable than polyester resin, allowing the use of lighter foam cores. Other shapers such as Clyde Beatty and Greg Loehr also were working in epoxy at the time. South African surfer Martin Potter tried an epoxy board in 1985 and immediately won a World Tour event. This led other top surfers like Brad Gerlach and Cheyne Horan to Bradbury epoxies, but they were ahead of the curve. There were advantages to epoxy, but also problems that went straight back to the same dilemmas that faced Bob Simmons, Joe Quigg, and Matt Kivlin in the early days of foam: Epoxy was more expensive, more difficult to work with, and a dinged epoxy board soaked up water instantly, forcing surfers to carry it straight out of the water and into the repair shop.

During the 1980s, there was a shift away from big performance waves like Sunset. Instead, surfers were trekking down the beach to the shorter and more intense breaks like Pipeline and Backdoor Pipeline. Waveriders like Curren, Tom Carroll, Dane Kealoha, and Johnny Boy Gomes surfed these waves with an aggression and depth that Herbie Fletcher and his pioneering friends only dreamed about in the 1960s on their mini-guns. Surfers were still riding giants at places like Waimea Bay, and these big days remained the last bastion for the single-fin, which some surfers felt went better in huge surf.

The New Surfing World

A major transition at both ends of the surfing scale came in 1992. This was the year Kelly Slater won the first of what is now eight world titles—and counting. An abnormally loose, limber, and focused surfer from Cocoa Beach, Florida, Slater was of average height and weight, but was able to do supernatural things on impossibly light and thin shortboards.

Naturally, it was Dave Parmenter who best summed up this New Surfing World. He theorized in *Surfer Magazine*: "Simply put, these modern boards won't float a 170-pound surfer, which is probably the average weight of the adult surfer. Another consideration: The gymnastic, slidey surfing engineered by these boards have left most of us behind for one reason or another. Although no one scoffs at the cleverness or dexterity of the New Surfing, I doubt it will ever make the crossover into mass acceptance. This new type of surfing is based on having a sensitive but driveless board in an utterly submissive state under your feet, surfing hotdog waves *and taking your weight off the board to do maneuvers.* But good, powerful surfing in overhead waves, the yardstick by which all surfers from the

'50s to the present can be measured, can only be achieved by putting your weight on the board and driving. What I'm saying is this: Don't look for that slidey shit at Sunset or G-land."

Slater dominated pro surfing in the 1990s. He often used that "slidey shit" in smaller surf, but also proved that Florida guys could handle Waimea, Pipeline, Grajagan, and anything else the ocean threw. Along the way, Slater established a new style of surfing—and that kind of surfboard Parmenter abhorred—which has been the vogue ever since.

Towing In

In the early 1990s, a trio of Hawaiian surfers—Laird Hamilton, Buzzy Kerbox, and Darrick Doerner—grew disenchanted by the endless flow of surfers coming to the islands and clogging the once-sacred breaks at Sunset Beach and Waimea Bay. Looking for new vistas and bigger thrills, these guys set off in an inflatable boat for a spot called Backyards. Here, they tried towing into waves that could not be caught by mortal men, no matter how strong they were or how big and thick a board they were riding. Hawaiian surfer Mark Foo had labeled these types of mammoth waves "The Unridden Realm" after taking off on a monster at Waimea in 1985 and nearly drowning.

Hamilton, Kerbox, and Doerner were on to something out at Backyards, riding conventional big-wave guns with no straps as they towed into dozens of waves in a session where before they would have been lucky to catch only one or two. As they refined their act, they got rid of the inflatable boat and switched to more powerful and maneuverable personal watercraft. And while they were snowboarding, a light

bulb lit: If they could ride huge mountains of snow on short, narrow snowboards, why couldn't they do the same on a mountain of moving water? Most big-wave boards were big because they needed length and thickness for paddling. As Matt Warshaw explained in *The Encyclopedia of Surfing*, "With paddling taken out of the equation by the tow-in launch, the new boards could be designed solely for on-wave performance, for doing turns and cutbacks in waves up to 50 feet or bigger. Board speed, as it turned out, had less to do with the momentum carried by a long board and more to do with being able to hold position in the wave's energy-rich 'pocket' area adjacent to the curl. Small tow-in boards, if designed properly, allowed surfers to remain in the pocket."

As part of a decade-long experiment in search of the ultimate tow-in ride, Hamilton worked with shapers to guillotine the size of his boards in 1993. By the end of the 1990s, the average tow-board measured just 7 feet long and 15 inches wide. Most tow-in surfboards were Thruster-style tri-fins, although some continued with twin-fins. The typical board tipped the scales at 25 pounds, Hamilton and friends often adding lead plates for stability and foot straps to aid leverage. Hamilton and his crew worked closely with shapers Dick Brewer and Gerry Lopez, but other top tow-in shapers included Maurice Cole, John Carper, and Jeff Timpone.

This trend in big-wave boards for tow surfing was the most radical design departure between the general acceptance of the Thruster and the closure of Clark Foam, the two mileposts of the post-modern world in surfboard design.

From Tri-Fin to Five-Fin

In between 1981 and 2006, the Thruster

Camaron Brujo, 7'2"

This beautiful Skip Frye–inspired design was shaped by Sebastian Galindo, Argentinean shaper and surfing champion. Adopted 2000.

Gerry Lopez Tow-In Board, 7'4"

Gerry shaped this board for himself in 2000 and surfed it many a time at Jaws. It's finished in classic Lopez colors. Adopted 2001.

Opposite:

Laird Hamilton's Quiver, 1990s

One of the biggest innovations of the post-Thruster era was the use of personal watercraft to tow surfers into giant waves that could not otherwise be caught bare-handed. Laird was the leader of this revolution. At some point, Laird and his strapped-in crew realized the big guns they were riding were big only to catch the wave. From there, tow boards got shorter and narrower and began to look more like snowboards. This is Laird with two of his tow-in quiver: One by master Gerry Lopez, the other by master Dick Brewer.
Photograph © Sylvain Cazenave

Tom Curren, 6'0"

This shortboard was Tom's personal ride. Adopted 2004.

cemented itself as the design choice for 90 percent of the surfboards made in California, Hawai'i, Australia, and elsewhere in the world. The Campbell Brothers had some success and followers with their five-fins, and there have been experiments with twin-fins and Fish and dozens of other designs, but most of the boards in today's waves are Thrusters.

In 1993, readers of *Australia's Surfing Life* magazine voted Californian Rusty Preisendorfer as the second-best shaper in the world, finishing runner-up to Merrick. Preisendorfer shaped boards for Shaun Tomson and Peter Townend in the mid-1970s, then made a series of Thrusters for a young Australian rookie named Marc Occhilupo, who subsequently shook up the world and engaged in an epic competitive rivalry with Tom Curren.

Preisendorfer founded Rusty Surfboard in 1985, using just a single "R" as his logo. Since 1988, he has shaped tens of thousands of boards for some of the world's best surfers, including Wes Laine, Kalani Robb, Taylor Knox, Serena Brooke, and big-wave riders Mike Parsons and Flea Virostko. In the 1990s, Preisendorfer's five-fin C5 model was hot stuff. In 2001, Florida surfer C. J. Hobgood rode a Rusty to a world title, and that year the R logo sold more than 14,000 boards and boasted some $40 million in surfboard and clothing sales. Preisendorfer explained his philosophy to Matt Warshaw in *The Encyclopedia of Surfing*: "I'm not interested in coming up with the next breakthrough in design. Trying to be consistent is what's most important."

Molded Boards by Surf Tech

Toward the end of the 1990s, yet another line of molded surfboards appeared in surf

Joe Curren, 6'4"

This was Joe Curren's personal board, part of an "Ultimate Curren quiver" adopted at the Summer Soiree Fundraiser for SurfAid. The other two pieces include Tom's personal 6'0" board and Pat's personal 9'2" board. Adopted 2004.

Mick Fanning
North Shore Gun,
7'10"

Shaped by DIID on October 23, 2001, for Mick's Hawaiian winter. It's signed by Mick and bears a great paint job. Adopted 2002.

Gary Linden Agave Swallowtail, 7'4"

Shaper Gary Linden crafted this board in 2000, inspired by a Skip Frye design. The agave was hand-harvested from the creeks of Mount Soledad in La Jolla, California. The wood was dried, then hand-glued into a blank, and hand-shaped by Gary. Adopted 2000.

Mentawai Island Board, 6'5"

During Fernando Aguerre's first trip to the Mentawai Islands in 2001, his good friend Cesar Colombo (several times Argentinean surfing champion) bought this board from a local surfer as a thank you present for Fernando. Crafted by an unknown shaper, the board is made of a local wood and features several folk art designs, seen in other wooden artifacts in the Islands. It's a one-of-a-kind board, with a very proper outline, boat-type rocker in both nose and tails, but very thin. Adopted 2001

shops, but this time the pop-outs made good. Since the 1960s, there had been resistance by surfers against the long legacy of hair-brained and/or brilliant molded innovations that bypassed the traditional surfboard hand-shaped from polyurethane foam and finished with fiberglass and resin. Pop-outs were not soulful, didn't work, or both. Over the years, the surfing world had tried molded boards from Robertson-Sweet, Diwan Surfboards, Bohemian, Inland Surfer, Sting Ray, Toes Over, WAVE Hollow, and a score of other brands. And at some point, all of them were discarded.

Now, along came Surf Tech. The man behind the name was Randy French, a veteran Santa Cruz shaper who had learned high-tech molding techniques and "vacuum bagging" while working on sailboards through the 1980s. French took a big gamble in applying these techniques to surfers, who had proven themselves too traditional to accept inexpensive pop-outs and yet also too cheap to pay for a quality molded board.

For the first time, Randy French got a pop-out right. And for the first time, a molded process was accepted by the most respected shapers and surfers. Surf Tech boards were made of epoxy and molded from precise designs crafted by famous shapers like Dale Velzy, Reynolds Yater, and Glen Minami. Through the 1990s and into the new century, Surf Tech was making waves and adding on a lot of famous names old and new—David Nuuhiwa, Pat Rawson, Robert August, Jim Banks, and more.

And still, some traditionalists argued that Surf Tech would sink the custom surfboard tradition. The argument against that argument, however, is that Surf Tech took care of all the "production" shaping, which

LAIRD

Laird

Whether paddling the English Channel, or dropping in on the largest waves found on earth, Laird Hamilton defines the ultimate waterman and for his exploits he demands the best equipment. Surftech is proud to offer the ultimate Standup Paddle Board.

TOW BOARD
Light, Medium, Heavy
N: 9 3/4"
M: 15 1/2"
T: 11 7/8"
TH: 1 1/2"

Sizes up to 107 inches. Composite construction makes these powerful, light weight paddles a superior product. The preferred paddles of Laird Hamilton, Wingnut and other watermen, these are specifically designed for Stand Up Paddlers of all levels.

**12' 1"
STANDUP
PADDLEBOARD**
N:21"
M: 31"
T:19 1/4"
TH: 4 1/8"

SURFTECH

TUFLITE
epoxy technology

WWW.SURFTECH.COM

31

Surf Tech Ad, 2006

took up the time of most shapers—even the great ones. Production boards are noncustom boards put up for sale in surf shops and other outlets. Surf Tech now covered anonymous production shaping, coming out with a product that was stronger and lighter than polyurethane and resin boards were acceptable to all, from pros to schmos. The shapers could stop doing production shaping and instead concentrate on the custom boards that most people mistakenly thought most shapers spent their time doing.

Surf Tech benefited by the 2005 closure of Clark Foam. After Blank Monday, all the custom-surfboard manufacturers scrambled to find blanks as Walker Foam ramped up in California and foreign companies came in with product and production facilities. Surf Tech, meanwhile, was ready to fill the vacuum with molded boards that didn't rely on polyurethane-foam-blank makers.

By 2006, Surf Tech was booming. Its warehouse in Huntington Beach was chock full of 10,000 Tuflite boards in more than 150 different sizes, shapes, and flavors. Depending on the season, the company was turning that inventory every couple of months, and there was a nonstop supply line of orders being sent to the Cobra factory in Thailand—a thoroughly modern, 180,400-square-foot facility that employed 2,400 people and produced 50,000 boards annually for Surf Tech and a variety of others. The pop-out was here to stay, and in 2004, Randy French was voted one of the 25 Most Powerful People in Surfing by *Surfer Magazine*.

Andrew Logreco, 2000s

Going against the tradition of hand-shaped surf-boards made from polyurethane foam and glassed with fiberglass and polyester resin, numerous manufacturers tried to produce and sell molded "popout" surfboards since the early 1960s. Many companies tried and many companies failed—until Santa Cruz shaper Randy French applied snow-board construction techniques to his SurfTech line. These high-tech boards are light and strong, and have found a significant niche in the booming surf-board market of the twenty-first century.
Photograph © Jeff Divine

Wayne Lynch Evolution, 8'0"
This was Wayne Lynch's personal Evolution board,
fitted with a 12-inch fin. Adopted 2002.

Blank Monday Reconsidered

Surf Tech inspired much controversy among traditionalists. But some people thought that anything that kept humans away from the toxic production of polyurethane surfboards was a good thing. That "Stinky" label put on surfboard shapers by the movie *Gidget* was truer than ever in the twenty-first century. For all their talk of alternative living, everyday surfers ride boards that are as petro-chemical-dependent as the worst SUV. It was exactly the toxicity of polyurethane-blank manufacturing that finally scared Grubby Clark out of business, and forced the surfboard industry to reconsider everything.

Clark had better business sense than Simon Anderson with his Thruster, and from the 1970s to December 5, 2005, Clark Foam boasted a near-monopoly on the production of polyurethane blanks in the United States and various other spots around the world. Clark ran his factory and business like Willie Wonka combined with Bill Gates. His was a closed shop, and Clark guarded his secrets and his numbers as he protected his monopoly—with great vengeance and furious anger. Since Harold Walker quit blowing blanks in the 1970s, Clark had built an efficient business supplying refined blanks in a wide variety of densities, shapes, and sizes to customers large and small. While Clark was accused of being the "Blank Nazi" because he would ruthlessly cut off any surfboard maker who dared to buy anything other than Clark, all who did business with him could not fault the precision of his customer service.

Thus, when Clark announced he was abruptly closing shop and not selling his business, hardware, or secrets, the surf industrial complex was left reeling.

Clark had many good reasons for shutting down, which he detailed in a

Mike Diffenderfer, 9'10"
Made of balsa and redwood, this was one of the last three boards Mike shaped. Adopted 2002.

Rob Machado's Channel Islands, 8'0"

Shaped by Al Merrick, this was Rob's personal Pipe board. Adopted 2003.

long, fax-ifesto sent out to shapers, magazines, gremmies, and anyone else who might care to listen. Clark was nearing retirement, he was the largest private landowner in Oregon, he had made enough money—and he didn't want to lose it all to a lawsuit brought by any governmental environmental bureaucracy or to an employee who contracted cancer from breathing in toxic fumes and dust forty hours a week.

So, after pioneering the industry and fifty years of blowing foam, Clark bade the surfing world goodbye, just like that. He left behind a business worth who knows what. No one knew how many blanks Clark produced a day or a week or a year, but the daily estimate of 1,000 proved true. Multiply that by 250 days a year with an

Continued on page 239

Derek Ho's Gun, 7'3"

This Pipeline big gun was surfed by World Champ Derek Ho in the winter of 2003. Adopted 2004.
Photograph by Larry Hammerness

Chew Surfboards Fish, 5'8"

This Fish was painted by artist Sli Dawg. Adopted from the Waterman's Ball Fundraiser for the Environment, 2003.

Shane Dorian's "JC," 7'3"

Shane donated this, his personal Pipe board, to a fundraiser to help Bethany Hamilton after her 2003 shark attack. Adopted 2003. Photograph by Larry Hammerness

Taylor Knox's Channel Islands, 6'2"

*This super-high-performance shortboard was Taylor's
personal board. He donated it to the Liquid Nation
Ball 2 fundraiser. Adopted 2004.*

Sofia Mulanovich's Channel Islands, 5'7"
This is one of Sofia Mulanovich's personal boards from her ISA and ASP World Championships year of 2004. An important board, from the very first ever Professional Surfing World Champion from Latin America, and inspiration to all Latins, but especially to Latinas. It's personally inscribed by Sofia to Fernando Aguerre. Adopted 2005.

Lisa Andersen's Channel Islands, 5'10"
Four-time World Champion Lisa Andersen's personal board from her 2004 season. Inscribed and autographed by Lisa to Fernando Aguerre: "For the man behind the (pink) pants." Adopted 2005.

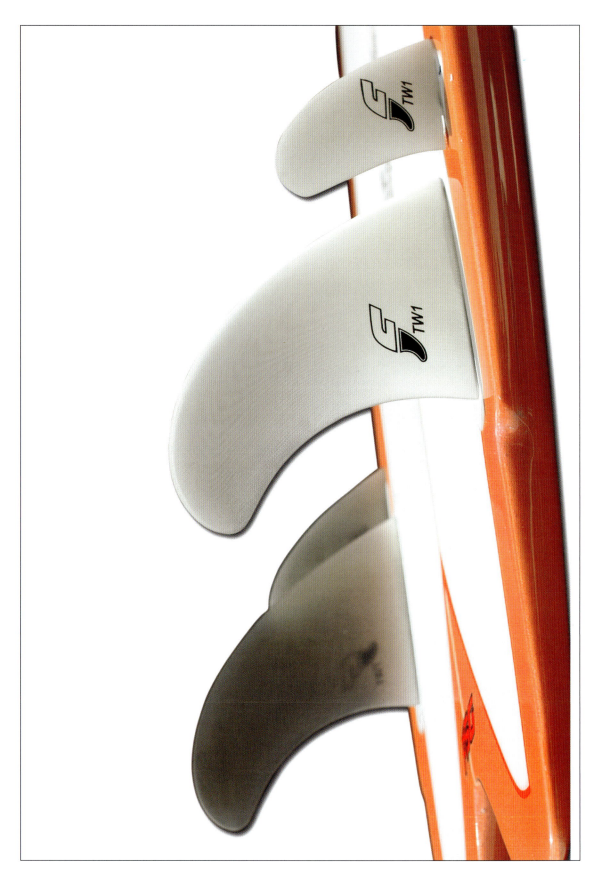

Mike Hynson Twinzer, 6'0"
This four-fin Twinzer was shaped and signed by Endless Summer legend Mike Hynson. Adopted from the Waterman's Ball Fundraiser for the Environment, 2004.

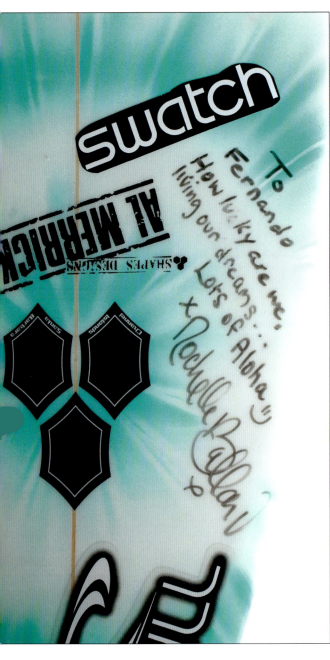

Rochelle Ballard's Channel Islands, 6'1"

This was Rochelle's personal board, shaped by Al Merrick. Adopted 2003.

Holly Beck's Rusty, 5'11"
Holly's personal board, shaped by Rusty.
Adopted 2003.

Continued from page 231
average price of $50 and that mountain of 250,000 to 300,000 blanks annually adds up to a mountain of business a lot larger than the Matterhorn at Disneyland.

Icons of a New Religion

Counting backward from 2006, the last twenty-five years of the evolution of the surfboard were bookended by two major upheavals. In 1981, it was design; in 2005, it was materials. Simon Anderson's Thruster defined the first. The closure of Clark Foam, the second.

With Clark Foam now history, the surfing world was forced to reconsider how it made boards, and what had been alternative ideas like Surf Tech and epoxy and even hemp and hardwoods all took a step upward in credibility.

In his "Thoroughly Modern Silly" manifesto, Dave Parmenter lamented the trend toward potato-chip boards that only specialized surfers could ride. But he also gave hope for the future. "The absurdity of the modern shortboard has had its benefits," he wrote. "It has cleared the path for an unprecedented renaissance of alternative surfcraft. And it's a healthy sign that most surfers are experienced and discerning enough not to be jerked around by the fads and fancy of 'shortboard fascism' in magazine hype."

Parmenter's early-1990s prophecy has proven true. You can see that flotilla of surfcraft, traditional and alternative, on any good day at Malibu. Eighty years after Tom Blake and Sam Reid first rode these waves and sixty years after Joe Quigg made the Easy Rider board for Darrilyn

Keala Kennely, 2000s

The surfer girls of the twenty-first century are using the new technology to boldly thrust themselves into situations where few female surfers have gone before. Here, Keala Kennely rides a Thruster at Telescopes in Sumatra. Photograph © Jeff Divine

Clark Foam Blanks, 2000s

Foam blanks on the racks at Clark Foam, ready to be moved out. Clark Foam was a bit like Willy Wonka's chocolate factory—closed off and secretive. The surfing industry wondered what went on in there like Slugworth wondered about the formula for Everlasting Gobstoppers. One of the most closely guarded secrets was the volume of blanks Clark produced annually. After Clark closed shop, some of that information was declassified and it came out that Clark was producing an astonishing 1,000 blanks a day. Photograph © Jeff Divine

Zanuck, Malibu remains one of the most popular surf spots in California and the world, a place where almost every imaginable kind of twenty-first-century surfboard is in style.

Sometimes at Malibu there will be as many as seven surfers riding one wave, and on that one wave you can find a lot of history all bumping a wide variety of rails: Thrusters and Fish, twin-fins and five-fins, high-tech longboards with one fin or three, and surfboard collectors out riding custom-made reproductions of Simmons spoons, Malibu chips, and Pacific System Homes Swastikas.

Looking out over Malibu on a good day—and it is one of the prettiest, most beguiling waves in the world when it wants to be—you have to wonder about the native Chumash teenagers, hundreds and even thousands of years ago. What did they do when confronted by a perfect southern swell unloading from Third Point to First Point? A wave is a wave and a human is a human and a thrill is a thrill, and it's easy to imagine the Chumash proto-gremmies risking the wrath of their elders and taking the family *tomol* canoe out for a spin in the surfline. The Chumash made great little canoes, and they lived an easy life there at "the place where the surf

Blank Monday, 2005

When Gordon Clark announced the complete, abrupt closure of Clark Foam, no one could believe that someone who had worked so hard to build up and dominate a market worth tens of millions of dollars would one day suddenly just say, "Hasta la vista!" But then this photo of some of the most prized Clark molds, all broken up and left at the dump, convinced the world that Clark meant all that he said. December 5, 2005, was a day that will live in infamy. Photograph © Jeff Divine

sounds loudly." Who knows how much design went into making those canoes better wave-riders, because a human is a human and a thrill is a thrill, and something in the human psyche just likes to ride waves.

Who knows, they might have been riding waves even before the Polynesians arrived in Owhyhee.

Andy Irons, 2005

There are three fins under Andy's board, but with the right pressure on his front foot and easing pressure on his back foot, he can ignore them all and bust his tail loose to make this cutback a little more radical. All a part of the New School revolution. Photograph © Jeff Divine

Andy Irons' Shortboard, 6'2"
This was one of Andy's personal shortboards surfed in the smaller surf during his 2003 World Championship–winning year. Adopted 2004.

Kelly Slater's Channel Islands, 7'2"
One of Slater's personal boards from his 2003 Hawaiian winter season. The board was snapped and repaired. Adopted 2004. Photograph by Larry Hammerness

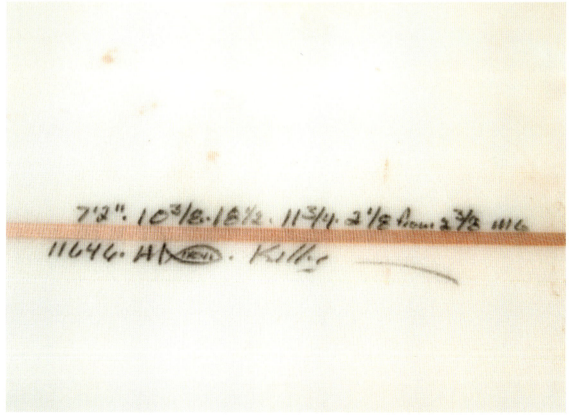

On the next page:
Kelly Slater, 2005

Float, float on. Kelly is the very model of a modern major surfing talent. His surfing from the early '90s into the twenty-first century has set the pace for an entire generation of smaller, lighter surfers—and smaller, lighter surfboards—that can go anywhere over, under, and around a wave. Photograph © Jeff Divine

Sunset on Another Perfect Day

A surfer leaves the water along the North Shore of Oahu. Under his arm are many thousands of years of cutting, edging, trimming, shaping, sanding, adjusting, tuning, trying and trying again— all in the effort of developing the perfect vehicle for riding waves. Photograph © Jeff Divine

Acknowledgments and Sources

First of all, thanks to Michael Dregni for boldly editing another book project of mine. After making him sweat through many edits on *Surfing USA!* I promised I would do this one faster and tighter, so of course I took two times too long and wrote two times too much. But I think I do that just to show what a literary ninja he is, hacking down a huge volume of words but still leaving the story intact. Not bad for someone from Saint Paul, Minnesota—wherever that is.

Thanks to Fernando Aguerre for giving us access to his home, castle, and epic surfboard collection. He allowed us to take all of his precious and semi-precious boards down from the walls and ceilings of his house, prop them up outside, and photograph them. We dinged the nose on that beautiful Brewer balsa gun and for that we will rot in hell, but we will rot knowing we did justice to his collection.

Juliana Morais photographed the boards, which was far from an easy task. Jeff Divine and others had warned me that shooting surfboards was tricky because of the angles and reflections—not a job to be handled by amateurs. Over two long days in winter 2006, Juliana worked with Gustavo Morais (no relation) and two other assistants to move, photograph, and replace more than 150 boards—some of them 14 feet tall and weighing more than 120 pounds. Juliana killed it.

Special thanks to the many surfing writers who came before me, carving out pieces of the surfboard's history, most of whom gave me permission beyond Fair Use in the name of the surfing legacy. Thanks to Spencer Croul from the Croul Family Foundation and the Surfing Heritage Foundation for publishing Gary Lynch's *Tom Blake: The Uncommon Journey of a Pioneering Waterman* and *Dale Velzy is Hawk* by Paul Holmes. Both books were invaluable in laying down the solid keel of a timeline that this book is built around.

Thanks to Steve Pezman, Scott Hulet, Jeff Divine, and the staff of *The Surfer's Journal*— the New Testament of surfing— for letting me root through their archives. Among the stories that were essential to compiling this history were "The Bob Simmons Enigma" by John Elwell in volume 3 number 1; "Hot Curl" by Craig Stecyk and "The Great Nose Riding Contest" by Tom Morey in 3/2; "Surf Drunk: The Wallace Froiseth Story" by Malcolm Gault-Williams in 6/4; "Moving Forward: A Greenough Scrapbook" curated by Paul Gross in 7/4; "The Life and Work of Richard Brewer" by Drew Kampion in 8/1; "Reinventing the Sport Part III—George Freeth" by Joel T

Smith in 12/3; "The Boards in My Life: George Downing's Epochal Surfboard Timeline" as told to Steve Pezman in 14/5; "Belief System: The Long, Strange Saga of the Bonzer" by Steve Barilotti in 13/2; "The Harbour Chronicles: A 60s Time Capsule" by Rich Harbour in 14/2; "Waterman Preston 'Pete' Peterson: A Life in Three Acts" by Craig Lockwood in 14/6; "The Foam Man: Dave Sweet's Story" as told to Steve Pezman in 15/2. I even quoted myself from some stories I did in *The Surfer's Journal*, including "The Price of Gas" in 12/2.

Through the miracle of the Internet I had access to www.legendarysurfers.com, where Malcolm Gault-Williams made available extensive research that made this book easier to write.

I also owe a debt to Stacy Peralta's *Riding Giants*; *Surfers: The Movie* by Michael Tomson; *Gotcha*; "Thoroughly Modern Silly" by Dave Parmenter in *Surfer*; and *Surfing: A History of the Ancient Hawaiian Sport* by James D. Houston and Ben Finney. For other source material I raided the archives at the Surfing Heritage Foundation for information and photos, so thanks to Dick Metz and Spencer Croul for building that institution and Tom Pezman and Barry Haun for maintaining it.

Also omniscient, omnipotent, and essential is Matt Warshaw's *The Encyclopedia of Surfing*, which put things like Dick Brewer's birthdate and the correct spelling of Rusty Preisendorfer at my fingertips.

For additional photos to flesh out the timeline of that surfboard collection, I relied on Desoto Brown and his staff at the Bishop Museum in Hawai'i. Keith Eshelman and Carey Weiss opened their surfboard sticker collection to me, and Mark Fragale sent me some visuals from his collection. Larry Hammerness came through at the last moment to photograph some last boards. And Jeff Divine helped illustrate surfboards at work as only he can do it.

Last but not least, my thanks to King Neptune for providing the waves that inspired all these men and women to get jiggy with it.

Index

About the Author and Contributors

A young Ben Marcus with his first surfboard, shaped by Doug Haut

Jeff Divine. Photograph by Russ Hoover

Fernando Aguerre

Ben Marcus

Ben Marcus grew up surfing in Santa Cruz in the 1970s, during a time when everyone wore puka shells and O'Neill Supersuits or Animal Skins, had long blond hair, and rocked out to Honk, Blind Faith, and Jimi Hendrix. After graduating from high school, Ben traveled the world in search of the perfect wave. In the 1980s, he wrote a short story about a surfing adventure on the Spanish Basque coast and submitted it to *Surfer* magazine. *Surfer* hired him as associate editor, where he remained for ten years, writing about many of the changes in surfing—the discovery of Maverick's, the debut of tow surfing, the arrival of the New School, and stars such as Lisa Andersen, Kelly Slater, and Laird Hamilton. Now here in the twenty-first century, Ben still surfs and travels as much as possible, writing for *The Surfer's Journal* and other publications. He is also the author of *Surfing USA!* and *Surfing and the Meaning of Life*, both published by Voyageur Press.

Jeff Divine

Jeff Divine is one of the world's most famed surfing photographers, bar none. He is the photo editor at *The Surfer's Journal*.

Juliana Morais

Dividing her time between her native Brazil and the United States, Juliana Morais is a photographer, filmmaker, and writer who contributes to ESPN Brazil and several surf and sports magazine worldwide. She is also a surfer.

Fernando Aguerre

Born and raised in Mar del Plata, Argentina, Fernando Aguerre has been surfing since age eleven. At twenty, when the Argentinean military dictatorship banned surfing, he founded the first Surfing Federation and fought to have the ban lifted, succeeding one year later. In 1984, he co-founded the surf brand Reef with brother Santiago, which they sold in 2005. He currently lives in La Jolla, California, where he's president of the International Surfing Association, serves in many humanitarian and environmental organizations, and continues to surf daily.

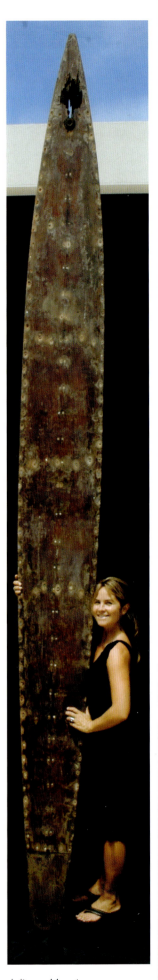

Juliana Morais